NORTHWESTERN UNIVERSITY STUDIES IN THE
SOCIAL SCIENCES

NUMBER II

NORTHWESTERN UNIVERSITY STUDIES IN THE SOCIAL SCIENCES NO. 2

SHAMANISM IN WESTERN NORTH AMERICA

A Study in Cultural Relationships

BY

WILLARD Z. PARK

NORTHWESTERN UNIVERSITY

1938

NORTHWESTERN UNIVERSITY

EVANSTON AND CHICAGO

NORTHWESTERN UNIVERSITY STUDIES

GEORGE BANTA PUBLISHING COMPANY, MENASHA, WISCONSIN

Contents

v

Preface

The present study has developed from a dissertation presented for the degree of Doctor of Philosophy at Yale University. That manuscript has been extensively revised with the inclusion of new and valuable comparative data. Revision has led also to a reformulation of the significance of the distributional evidence for the basic problems involved in the inferential reconstruction of native history in western North America.

The descriptive data on shamanism presented here were collected in the course of three summers spent in making an ethnographic study of the Paviotso Indians in western Nevada. Work during the summer of 1933 was made possible through the generosity of Mr. H. U. Brandenstein of San Francisco. I am grateful to him for making it possible for me to gain my first experience in field work and for continued encouragement and interest. Investigations during the following two seasons were made under the auspices of the Institute of Human Relations at Yale University. The financial support which enabled me to add materially to my knowledge of Paviotso culture is deeply appreciated.

The gathering of the material and the preparation of this study have benefited from the suggestions and encouragement of my teachers and colleagues. Above all I wish to express my gratitude to Dr. Edward Sapir and Dr. Leslie Spier, who, by their inspiration, encouragement, and helpful suggestions in the course of field work and in the preparation of the present study, contributed materially to my understanding of ethnological problems. Dr. Melville J. Herskovits's many valuable criticisms during the course of revision, and his unfailing encouragement to publish this venture in the field of anthropological theory are deeply appreciated. Dr. Robert H. Lowie was kind enough to read the manuscript and make suggestions for improvement.

Many people have generously contributed to make up the serious deficiencies in the published accounts of shamanism in western North America. I wish to extend my thanks here to all who so kindly placed unpublished field notes at my disposal. Specific acknowledgment is made where these important additions enter the discussion.

Lastly, it is with pleasure that I acknowledge the extremely large obligation due my wife, Susan Park. Her advice, assistance, and encouragement both in the field and in the preparation and revision that culminated in the present study have been invaluable to me. Her unpublished field notes on the Atsugewi and Cahuilla have also filled in a number of gaps in the literature. In all, her contribution to the finished work has been great indeed.

The phonetic symbols used in the recording of Paviotso terms follow the simpler system of the *Phonetic Transcription of Indian Languages* (Smithsonian Misc. Coll., 66, no. 6, 1916).

W. Z. P.

I. The Problem

For several decades the religions of the American Indian tribes have provided data for the anthropologist bent on reconstructing the history and interrelationships of New World cultures. Notable studies in this field have displayed a wide variety of interests and aims, ranging from an intensive investigation of growth in a single tribal religion to an analysis of the interrelationships, practices, and beliefs on a continental scale. Still others have sought to reconstruct the growth, including relative chronological sequences, of ceremonies or entire religions in a more or less culturally homogeneous area. Whatever the specific goal and scope of these studies may be, it is either explicitly stated or implicitly recognized that the empirical data of geographical distribution, in the absence of more direct evidence such as documentary accounts of past events, afford an important body of knowledge for inferring the history of religions along with other cultural developments.

The distributional study of even simple generalized customs and beliefs yields evidence of the various interrelationships of cultures during their growth. Just as in the reconstruction of the history of more complex institutions, it is not necessary, and in fact it may be impossible, to determine the chronological sequence of accretion. Knowledge of the divergent sources and spatial relationships of several elements forming the complex does indicate, however, the interconnections among localized unique cultures. Without any attempt to postulate time-sequences, this may be considered a legitimate approach to the problems of culture history.

Shamanism in the New World presents an example of relatively simple and undifferentiated practices and beliefs which have wide but differing distributions. Moreover, the nearly universal occurrence in the Western Hemisphere of this type of religion suggests a respectable antiquity, at any rate, for some of the elements of the complex. Possibly, as Kroeber[1] suggests, shamanism may have been part of the cultural equipment of the first settlers in

---

[1] Kroeber, *Anthropology*, 349; *American Culture and the Northwest Coast*, 2.

the New World. This, however, does not argue that the simple elements forming the complex are identical throughout the Western Hemisphere. A merely superficial examination of North American shamanism reveals quite striking differences in content, in meaning, and in the way practices and beliefs are combined with other customs. Years ago, Dixon pointed out certain of these distinctions in the attitudes and customs of the New World shamans. The local variations evident in that brief survey include, among others, differences in means of acquiring supernatural power, the variety in the functions and the performances of the shamans, and their position and influence in society.[2] Important distinctions in practices clearly setting off one part of aboriginal California from another were recognized by Kroeber.[3] Again, Spier, in appraising recently the place of the Klamath in western North America, has precisely defined the distribution of certain of the elements in the shamanistic complex of this region.[4] It is evident that despite the possible considerable age and relative simplicity of shamanism in the New World, we are dealing with a locally varying amalgam of historically heterogeneous traits. Accordingly, a study of the practices and beliefs of a particular tribe in reference to their spatial setting should reveal at least some of the cultural relationships contributing to the development of the localized complex.

SCOPE OF THE PROBLEM

The goal of the present study will be to ascertain those interrelationships of tribal cultures reflected in the geographical distributions of the elements found in a single localized shamanistic complex. The practices and beliefs of the shamans among the Paviotso or Northern Paiute of western Nevada will be considered in their distributional setting in order to indicate the cultural connections contributing to the growth of that complex.

In order to focus attention on the elements which are to be analyzed in their spatial relationships, an account of Paviotso practices and beliefs will first be presented. The distribution of

[2] Dixon, *Some Aspects of the American Shaman.*
[3] Kroeber, *The Religion of the Indians of California,* 327–334; *Handbook,* 851–855.
[4] Spier, *Klamath Ethnography,* 224 f.

these elements will then be traced among the neighboring tribes of the Great Basin, the Plateau, California, and several of the so-called Western Rancheria[5] tribes of the non-pueblo Southwest. The data thus presented will suggest some of the cultural relationships among the several tribes of this region. In addition, this evidence should enable us to appraise certain of the tribal and regional differences and similarities with reference to several important historical problems in western North America.

One of these more persistent questions in the cultural history of this region is that of the relationship of Great Basin cultures with those of the surrounding areas of central California, the Plateau, and the Plains. It is manifestly impossible to determine on the basis of only one phase of culture, such as shamanism, the interdependence or individuality of a group of cultures. Nevertheless, a precise statement of the Paviotso position, and so far as possible that of other Basin tribes, in shamanistic practices both in contrast and in relation to the neighboring areas will suggest more accurately than has been possible to date the extent of historical independence of and connection with the surrounding cultures.

It should be clearly understood that limiting the present study to a particular area of western North America carries no implication of historical autonomy for that region. Unquestionably, an appreciable number of the elements found in this area occur widely elsewhere in the New World and also in Asia. Thus the distribution of certain practices within this area will not exhaust all the possibilities of interrelationships. Although continental and intercontinental distributions yield evidence of suggestive historical connections, the growth of a local complex can be inferred from a detailed examination of more limited spatial interrelationships. In this study, therefore, I shall analyze the shamanistic phenomena of an arbitrarily delimited area, always recognizing

[5] This term is used by Spier to designate the group which "includes the tribes lying between the western Pueblos and the Colorado river, i.e., Navaho, Western Apache, Pima, Papago, Havasupai, Yavapai, Walapai, and others." *Problems Arising from the Cultural Position of the Havasupai*, 214.

Not all the tribes of this group will be considered in this study, for data on shamanism from some are extremely scanty, whereas with others, as in the case of the Navaho, the heavy overlay of Pueblo ceremonialism as yet obscures the precise extent of shamanism in the religious life.

possibilities of intrusive influences from surrounding cultures.

The position of the present undertaking in relation to other distributional studies of shamanistic practices in western North America should be clarified. In assessing the position of the Klamath among the cultures of western North America, Spier has given by far the most thorough and exhaustive analysis of the geographical range of certain practices.[6] Although additional material available since the publication of *Klamath Ethnography* modifies few of Spier's conclusions, a re-examination of the data and the use of the new material should shed light on those cultural connections reflected in the growth of the Paviotso complex. Further, whatever unique features characterize the practices of these people, perhaps those of the Great Basin as a whole should emerge from the distributional data.

Some of the methodological difficulties besetting such an historical study as the present one should not pass unremarked. In the first place, it is generally recognized that the growth of culture through the processes of diffusion is not mechanical; that there are powerful, but often subtle, factors that determine the selection and modification of traits in the course of the development of a complex or of a total civilization. In the case of the shamanistic complex under consideration here, it can be shown that elements found among the Paviotso enter into different combinations and are variously interpreted in the religions of neighboring peoples. It follows, then, that the conditions under which transmission takes place and the cultural setting into which new elements are fitted are of the utmost importance in accurately reconstructing a detailed and fully satisfactory history of a tribal culture. But empirical knowledge of these factors in societies that have no means of recording in reasonably permanent form events which lead to change, can be derived, as Radin has demonstrated,[7] only from the study of the actual conditions under which each case of borrowing takes place. Radin is unquestionably right when he insists that documents recorded by actual participants in events yield valuable direct evidence of history, but it is imposing un-

---

[6] Spier, *Klamath Ethnography*, 239–279. I wish to acknowledge with gratitude my debt to this study. It will be evident in the following pages that I have drawn upon it heavily for suggestions and guidance in procedure and for material.

[7] Radin, *A Sketch of the Peyote Cult*, 1, 22; *Method and Theory of Ethnology*, 186–238.

justifiable limits on historical reconstruction when evidence of only these recent events is admitted; that other cases of borrowing have not been recorded in such satisfactory detail does not argue that they should be ignored. Here the historian of culture is confronted with the need for sober analysis of the data of geographical distribution in order to derive the maximum of historical inference warranted by the information, avoiding pretentious claims for completeness and chronology. If we recognize, then, that reconstruction of the unverified events of the past in terms of generalized situations may often be misleading, it will be more realistic simply to regard diffusion here as an accomplished fact and to confine attention to the task of determining the cultural connections in the area under consideration without postulating unauthenticated conditions of diffusion and assimilation.

Naturally, this does not mean that all elements in the complex are to be weighted alike in such an historical reconstruction. It must be recognized that there are important differentials in the diffusion of separate elements as well as of systems of cultures, that one trait may spread rapidly over a wide area while another custom or practice, equally old, may be transmitted to only a limited number of cultures.[8] Thus it cannot be denied that the transmission of shamanistic practices in western North America has been facilitated in some cases and in others inhibited by numerous cultural and geographical factors.[9] It is no longer possible, however, to determine the precise circumstances which in one tribe facilitated the adoption of a new practice and in another culture caused its rejection. Certainly this consideration alone gives a dubious validity to any time-sequence inferred only from distributional evidence. In view of these limitations on the inferential reconstruction of history, therefore, the present study will be restricted to the determination of the interrelationships of the Paviotso with the surrounding cultures, so far as the evidence warrants. Nevertheless, the operation of certain factors favoring

[8] It is recognized that anthropologists are usually aware of these crucial points. In fact, the general formulations of the problems involved in culture-borrowing nearly always emphasize the factors controlling the spread of cultures and traits. Frequently, however, the same scholars neglect or ignore these powerful differentials in making specific historical reconstructions.

[9] Sapir has discussed a number of the conditions that are responsible for differences in rates of diffusion. *Time Perspective*, 30 f.

or limiting the processes of borrowing cannot be ignored entirely, for from the uniqueness of a complex which in terms of content can be duplicated in several neighboring tribes, it is evident that they have had an important rôle in the selection and interpretation of traits.

Still another problem involving these differentials in the rate of diffusion is that of the weighting or determining of what may be called the historical value of cultural elements or complexes. It should be recognized that the distribution of one element or a particular cluster of beliefs and practices may indicate closer historical connection than can be inferred from the geographical range of another trait or complex. An example will clarify this point. Among a considerable number of tribes in western North America, shamanistic power is customarily secured by a deliberate quest. The frequently recurring association of several practices and beliefs in the "power quest" suggests a higher degree of relationship among the people following this practice than is indicated by the distribution of such a belief as that in which supernatural power is derived from animal spirits. Often, of course, the closer connection inferred on this basis may result from a more recent development and spread of the complex; but this chronological sequence cannot always be verified. On the other hand, in an appreciable number of other instances there is no justification at all for an assumption of time-relationships. It is evident, then, that although relatively complex traits or complexes often offer a basis for inferring close relationship among the cultures where they are found, such reconstructions do not depend alone on this factor, for apparently simple practices in some instances are likewise of considerable value in determining past cultural connections. Clearly, the historical value of culture traits rests upon the several factors that are responsible for differences in both the rate of diffusion and the conditions under which selection and assimilation take place. At present, criteria are not available for judging differentials in historical usefulness of the distributional data of institutions and customs. Possibly, exhaustive critical studies of many culture complexes under carefully analyzed conditions of transmission may illuminate this problem so vital to the inferential reconstruction of culture history. These considerations make it imperative, therefore, to recognize that at least a judicious weighting of distributional evidence is vitally important in making historical inferences, for the mechanical use of such data may lead to results which are quite as misleading as unsupported theorizing.

These tantalizing obstacles in the path of accurate and faithful history are often complicated by a meagerness of data at important points. At other times a decided unevenness of treatment, even where materials are reasonably full, seriously handicaps distributional studies. It must be evident that inferential reconstructions cannot be expected to fill many of the lacunae in our knowledge of the past. It is clear, then, that it is possible to define here only approximately those interrelationships of cultures in western North America suggested by the distributional evidence. The difficulties inherent in this study are, of course, those common to all attempts at reconstruction that follow this or similar procedures. They are still no less crucial in assessing the validity of the history which may be inferred from the evidence that is to be presented.

Still another limitation placed on the present study deserves a brief remark. Without doubt, such an analysis as is proposed here neglects many important problems involving the subjective side of religious experiences in these cultures. Unquestionably, shamanism offers a fascinating field for psychological investigation of culture and is, moreover, rich in possibilities for a fruitful examination of the interrelationships of personality and culture. It is not necessarily true that these problems have no place in an historical study, for many of the subjective attitudes and components of personality may eventually prove to be as much the product of cultural development as institutions and customs. At the present time, however, material is not available for a consideration of the historical movements in these subtler phases of cultures.

Finally, we must not ignore the importance that individuals may have played in the growth of the complex that is to be analyzed here. Radin has assigned to the North American shaman the task of systematizing and interpreting religious ideas,[10] but

[10] Radin, *Religion of North American Indians*, 269 f.

it is not apparent that shamans everywhere in the New World have performed this function to the same degree. Nevertheless, the changes in the shamanistic practices and beliefs have in each tribe resulted from the borrowing, the interpretations, and the inventions of novel ideas by individual shamans. A thorough study of borrowing processes must take into account such significant events and people. At the present time, however, knowledge of the contributions made by individual shamans to the totality of Paviotso practice is irretrievably lost to us. Therefore, although it is vitally important to bear in mind that these forces are ever present in making history, the limitations imposed on this study minimize the necessity for unverifiable assumptions of individuals, events, or chronology.

DEFINITION OF SHAMANISM

The great diversity of practices and beliefs presented by a survey of shamanism does not readily yield a clear definition of the term. In fact, shamanism usually has been defined descriptively, often in terms of the practices of a particular region. That this procedure is subject to error is evident when it is realized that in one society the shaman may have certain priestly functions, in another his duties relate only to curing. Laufer has shown that the word itself is an old term in the Turkish-Tungusian languages.[11] Frequently, we find that shamanism is defined largely by eastern Siberian practices. In clarifying the differences in current usage and in order to arrive at a definite formulation of the term for this study, it is interesting to review briefly several of the definitions prevailing in the literature.

Shamanism is defined by MacCulloch in terms of the functions of the shaman. According to this statement, the shaman is regarded as one who has undifferentiated priestly, prophetic, and magico-medical functions. Although it is recognized that the shaman exercises certain priestly functions, his main powers are connected with healing and divination. "He has direct intercourse with spirits and actual (bodily or spiritual) access to the spirit-world. All his magical arts are done by virtue of his power over

---

[11] Laufer, *Origin of the Word Shaman*, 361.

or influence with spirits."[12] The shaman is accordingly distinguished by his active relations to the spirit world, not by his knowledge of esoteric doctrines and rituals.

Swanton distinguishes two classes of mediators between the world of spirits and the world of men, shamans, and priests. The shaman's authority is entirely dependent on individual ability. The priests are those who act "in some measure for the tribe or nation, or at least for some society."[13] This clean-cut differentiation of priests and shamans does not hold everywhere, for in some cultures, such as those of the Northwest coast, shamans exercise certain priestly functions, although in this respect they may be overshadowed by other officials, e.g., the chiefs who act as priests in the performances of the secret societies among the Tlingit, Haida, and Kwakiutl.

A similar distinction between shaman and priest has been made by Wissler. The priest is regarded as one who has knowledge of the rituals and leads ritualistic performances; his office is therefore primarily dependent upon learning, not upon direct personal experience with supernatural forces. The shaman, on the other hand, works by virtue of his possession of supernatural power. With this power he usually performs curative rites and acts as a prophet and seer.[14] This formulation likewise ignores the important points at which there is overlapping, for the appreciable body of knowledge gained by experience or apprenticeship is often an important part of the equipment distinguishing the shaman from his fellowmen.

One point is held in common by all these definitions: the shaman in all cases is one who has direct relationships with spirit powers in contrast to the priest who fills his office largely by virtue of his knowledge of rituals. Among some peoples, however, there is a certain overlapping of the functions belonging to the two offices. Some writers tend to regard as shamans all who experience personal contact with supernatural powers. A characteristic definition of this type is that given by Dixon, who applied the term "to that motley class of persons found in every savage community, who

[12] MacCulloch, in Hastings' Encyclopaedia of Religion and Ethics, Vol. XI, 441–442.
[13] Swanton, article "Shamans and Priests" in Handbook of American Indians, Vol. II, 522–524.
[14] Wissler, The American Indian, 197, 200–201.

are supposed to have closer relations with the supernatural than other men, and who, according as they use the advantage of their position in one way or another, are the progenitors alike of the physician and the sorcerer, the prophet, the teacher, and the priest."[15]

The possession of power alone, however, does not necessarily distinguish the shaman from other men. In some tribes, almost everyone has visionary experiences in which some power to control supernatural forces is acquired. Under these conditions, the shaman may be regarded as one upon whom more than the usual amount of power is bestowed, and is so differentiated in native thought. Usually, the recipient of the power employs it for desirable social purposes, such as the curing of disease or the charming of game. Here shamanism is but a matter of degree; the shaman has the stronger power which enables him to perform certain functions in contrast to weaker powers of the laity. Moreover, the use of power for the good of others differentiates the shaman from the man who manipulates supernatural spirits for selfish ends. Of course this is an arbitrary distinction, for it is often difficult to distinguish between social and purely selfish interests.

For the purposes of this study, the shaman is one who acquires supernatural power through direct personal experience. This power is generally manipulated in such a way as to be a matter of concern to others in the society. Accordingly, the practice of witchcraft may be as important a part of shamanism as the curing of disease or the charming of game in a communal hunt. We will designate by the term shamanism, then, all the practices by which supernatural power may be acquired by mortals, the exercise of that power either for good or evil, and all the concepts and beliefs associated with these practices.

[15] Dixon, *Some Aspects of the American Shaman*, 1.

II. Paviotso Shamanism

INTRODUCTION

The material on Paviotso shamanism presented in this section was collected in the course of ethnographic field investigations carried on by the writer over a period of three summers.[1] Before the coming of the whites, the Paviotso roamed over the semi-arid country of western Nevada and Honey Lake Valley in California. In the winter and spring they lived on the shores of the lakes of this region—Pyramid, Humboldt, Carson and Walker Lakes of Nevada, and Honey Lake in California. Probably at no time did the population exceed three thousand. At the present time there are nearly a thousand full-blooded and half-breed Paviotso living on the Pyramid Lake, Walker River, and Fallon reservations and in the small colonies at the Nevada towns of Reno, Yerington, and Lovelock.

The Paviotso or Northern Paiute living largely in western Nevada, belong to the Mono-Paviotso branch of Shoshonean-speaking peoples. Although dialectically and geographically very close to the Paiute of Surprise and Owens valleys, the Nevada bands form an ethnic unit quite distinct from their linguistic relatives in California.[2]

Under aboriginal conditions, the Paviotso were on friendly and intimate terms with the Northern Paiute of Surprise and Owens valleys in California, to whose language their own is closely related. The Washo, living immediately to the west, were peaceful but not friendly. Contacts with these people were infrequent. Constant warfare was carried on with the Pit River Indians of California, who were their traditional enemies. The northeastern Maidu were also unfriendly and often came into conflict with the Paviotso. Other people in northeastern California and southern

---

[1] A preliminary account based on the first summer's field work was published in 1934 (see Park, *Paviotso Shamanism*). Material obtained on subsequent trips added considerable data, modified some, and corroborated other aspects of the earlier statement. The present account of Paviotso practices, although offered as a more accurate picture, is but a summary. It is hoped that it will be possible in the near future to publish the detailed material as a part of a rounded account of Paviotso culture. This chapter can thus be regarded essentially as a skeletonized version of Paviotso practice and belief.

[2] Kelly, *Surprise Valley Paiute*, 70–73; Steward, *Owens Valley Paiute*, 235–237.

Oregon were known to the Nevada Paviotso only through their Surprise Valley friends. To the east, the Paviotso had contacts solely with their immediate neighbors, the Western Shoshoni. Their relations with these people, however, were never so intimate and friendly as with the Northern Paiute of California. The Paviotso claim that the Bannock once were associated with them, but that these people moved east in search of the buffalo. It is doubtful whether the Paviotso and Bannock were in communication with each other in the period immediately preceding white occupation. The Southern Paiute, the Ute groups, and other Shoshonean peoples of the Basin were not known to the Paviotso.

The Paviotso have a culture which is usually regarded as Great Basin, but our present knowledge of this region is far too scanty to enable us to state just how typical of Basin culture are Paviotso customs. In their economic life, the wild products afforded by the habitat are utilized. Hunting, fishing, and gathering wild seeds and roots provide the food supply. Houses are simple but well-constructed, mat-covered and dome-shaped. Before the recent introduction of the Plains type of garments, clothing was negligible— a breechclout for men, a single apron in front or a double one front and back for the women, supplemented in the case of both sexes by woven skin robes and moccasins.

The social, political, and religious phases of Paviotso culture are likewise simple. The family is the basic unit in the social, as well as the economic, life. The five Paviotso bands are loose, localized, named groups with head-men or chiefs who have only advisory functions. Ceremonial performances are meager and mostly confined to shamanistic curing.

A great deal of the Paviotso culture has disappeared under reservation conditions. This is particularly true of economic life and material culture. Nevertheless, many social customs and religious beliefs and practices persist. Shamans are still common, and curing performances are frequent. Consequently, it has been possible to obtain accounts of a living religion from both shamans and laymen.

A brief statement on the sources of the material presented here may give some notion both of the value of these data as a basis for an accurate picture of the Paviotso complex and of their usefulness for comparative purposes. Three shamans, Dick Mahwee and Joe Green at Pyramid Lake, and Rosie Plummer at Schurz on the Walker River reservation, were very willing and intelligent informants. Joe Green spoke English sufficiently well so that an interpreter was not required. An interpreter was necessary in working with both Dick Mahwee and Rosie Plummer. However, Dick Mahwee had spent several months in 1914 at the University of California Museum of Anthropology at San Francisco, acting as an informant in linguistic studies. This was a number of years before he became a shaman. As a result of his experience in San Francisco, he was well aware of, and sympathetic toward, the aims of ethnographic investigation. He had acquired also a limited knowledge of English which enabled him to check the translations of the interpreter. Frequently he stopped the interpreter in his English renditions and insisted on a re-phrasing or a correction of a misstatement. This, coupled with a very sincere desire for accuracy, gives to the material recorded from Dick Mahwee a high degree of creditability.

Daisy Lopez, who acted as the interpreter for Rosie Plummer, was very intelligent and sympathetic. She had an unusually good command of English, in addition to a far better knowledge of the Paviotso language than is usual among the younger generation. The usefulness of Daisy Lopez was not, however, confined to interpreting. As she was the daughter of Rosie Plummer and had been constantly with her mother, except for a few years spent at school, she was well informed on much of the aboriginal culture.

As has been noted, Joe Green did not require an interpreter. He at one time acquired power, but through a misadventure described below had lost it. Joe was one of the most intelligent and conscientious of all the informants and he took an unusually active interest in the work of recording cultural data. Well liked and respected by his fellow tribesmen, he was able to obtain the help of others when information of which he was unsure was requested of him. This service was of considerable value, as many of the older people disliked talking to strangers. Joe Green thus made it possible to tap a number of rich sources of material which would have otherwise remained unexploited.

Important as shamans were in giving information, they did not provide all the data on this phase of the culture. Full accounts of shamanistic beliefs and practices were recorded from six well-informed laymen, about half of whom spoke English, the others requiring interpreters. Finally, many of the statements made by both shamans and non-shamans were checked with some fourteen or fifteen additional informants from whom only fragmentary material on shamanism could be obtained.

Before the intrusion of the whites, the Paviotso of western Nevada lived in five named, loosely organized, localized bands. The geographical centers for these semi-nomadic groups were the five lakes of the region: Pyramid, Walker, Humboldt, and Carson Lakes in western Nevada, and Honey Lake a few miles west of the Nevada-California state line. Data on all aspects of the culture were recorded from informants belonging to each of these localized groups. A careful scrutiny of this material, both that on shamanism and on the other phases of the culture, shows no significant cultural differences among the bands. Differences that appear in the accounts—and this is particularly true of the data on shamanism—seem to be the result of individual interpretation rather than cultural distinctions among local groups. In short, the loose localized bands of the Paviotso prove on investigation not to be separate cultural units. Therefore the Paviotso embracing these five so-called bands will be treated here as an ethnic unit.

The most important aspect of the religious life of the Paviotso is shamanism. There are other religious beliefs and observances also, as for example praying to the sun for success in the hunt, for relief from pain, for protection against the evil consequences of dreams, or for well-being, belief in the efficacy of charms, and the slightly religious tinge of the round dances. But all of these play a minor rôle in the religion of the Paviotso compared to shamanistic beliefs and practices.

The world in which the Paviotso live is full of animate beings unseen in a workaday experience. The spirits of animals, birds, and insects, spirits that live in certain caves in the mountains, water-babies that live in water-holes and in the lakes, the spirits of the wind, clouds and thunder, all can talk to man and assist him in his struggle to gain a living, to preserve health, and to cure sickness.

It is in respect to the last activity that the shaman is an out-standingly important member of Paviotso society. Although a man can acquire supernatural power which will enable him to be a successful hunter or a lucky gambler, these ends may be accomplished more simply by praying to the sun, or before the hunt by dreaming where game is to be found, or by use of charms. The shaman may also have the power to control weather, but this is not usually exercised for the good of the community. Rather, his demonstration of control over the elements seems to prove the shaman's *rapport* with powerful spirits, which give him power to cure the sick and heal the wounded. It is, then, the supernatural inspiration and assistance which enable one either to draw out the cause of illness or to go in search of the lost soul of a patient that is pre-eminent in the Paviotso mind as giving meaning and importance to the acquisition and exercise of shamanistic power. It should be noted that a shaman who has power to doctor the sick is called puhágɔm. This term is not used to designate people who possess supernatural powers for hunting, gambling, or warfare. There is no term for such power or for the people who enjoy it. However, supernatural aid in these latter functions is of the same sort and from the same source—spirits of animals, birds, etc.—as that acquired by a shaman. All supernatural power is, in theory, of the same order, but it is the possession of strong power to be exercised in the function of curing that is important in Paviotso ideology. The other objectives can be, and in fact most frequently are, accomplished satisfactorily, without spirit aid. Only curing depends directly upon power.

Source of Shamanistic Power

The spirit beings which are everywhere in the Paviotso world are the sources of supernatural power. Spirits of the fauna, spirits from certain mountains and of rocks, as well as the elements, bestow on individuals the power (puhá) through which sickness is controlled and cured. In addition to securing power from these spirits, shamans also derive supernatural aid from ghosts of the dead (sa'ab°) and from the dwarf-like creatures called water-babies that live in certain water-holes, lakes, and water-serpents thought to inhabit the lakes.

Indians were put here on this earth with trees, plants, animals, and water, and the shaman gets his power from them. One shaman might get his power from the hawk that lives in the mountains. Another may get his power from the eagle, the otter, or the bear. A long time ago, all the animals were Indians (they could talk). I think that is why the animals help the people to be shamans. Some strong shamans get their powers from the sun. (Joe Green)

Anyone can get to be a shaman by dreaming. In the dreams, spirits such as those from the eagle, bear, owl, snake, antelope, deer, mountain sheep, mole, or falling star appear. The spirit that comes in the dreams is the shaman's power. It helps him to doctor sick people. (Harry Sampson)

It is not altogether clear whether the animal spirits are conceived to be those of the species or of a single animal. One statement would seem to indicate that it is a spirit of the species that confers power.

When a shaman gets his power from the otter it means that the spirit is from many otters. The chief otter spirit tells the man to be a good doctor. It is this main otter that cannot be seen by the common people. He is the one that makes a man a shaman. He lives in a certain place in the water. Only the shaman can see him there. He knows where the otter is. He dreams about the otter and after a while he learns where the otter lives. (Joe Green)

This point was not carefully checked with other informants, but it would seem that the above statement formulates fairly accurately the norm of Paviotso belief in the animal and bird spirits that bestow shamanistic powers.

Several informants described the water-babies that are also believed to be a source of supernatural power.

Some shamans get their power from the water-babies. They are the only people who can talk to them. They tell the rest of the people not to make fun of water-babies. These shamans can take the water-babies out of the lake.

The water-babies came to life by their own power. They formed themselves. Some water-babies live in water-holes, and these holes never dry up. People call these water-babies the "breath of the water-holes." There is a cool breeze all the time in the mountains where they live. They have the power to cause wind to blow, even a very strong wind. The wind is their breath.

There are also women in the lakes where the water-babies live. These women are like the water-babies. They have the same power. Big serpents live in the lake, too. Like the water-babies, these serpents have strong power. They give power to some shamans. (Rosie Plummer)

A somewhat different statement of the source of shamanistic power, probably due to individual interpretation, was given by Dick Mahwee.

The Indian doctor gets his power from the spirit of the night. This spirit is everywhere. It has no name. There is no word for it. The Indians hold this spirit so sacred that they are afraid if they had a name for it the spirit would be angry. No one has ever dared give it a name.

Eagle and owl do not give a shaman power.[3] They are just messengers that bring instructions from the spirit of the night. Some doctors have water-babies for their messengers. They are called when the shaman doctors. They do not give him his power; they only carry messages from the spirit of the night. When the shaman is treating a patient he calls for the water-babies and they bring him instructions from the spirit.

At the time that the spirit of the night gives power for doctoring, it tells the shaman to ask for help from the water-babies, eagle, owl, deer, antelope, bear or some other bird or animal.

When shamans get power it always comes from the night. They are told to doctor only at night. This power has nothing to do with the moon or stars. I knew one woman who used the sun, moon, and stars for her power. I saw her fill her pipe and just as the sun came up she puffed and started to smoke. I saw her do this several times. I watched her closely but she did not use matches. Her power lighted her pipe.

A similar formulation of the spirit of the night as the source of power was made by Joe Green, also at Pyramid Lake.

There are two nights. The second one comes behind the night that everybody sees. This second night is under the darkness. It tells the shaman where the pain is and what caused the sickness. When the second night comes it makes the shaman feel that he is a doctor. The power is in him to doctor. Only shamans can see this second night. The people can only see the darkness. They cannot see the night under it.

In other statements, Joe Green insisted that power came from the spirits of animals; and, as has been noted, his own power came from the otter. This view of the source of supernatural aid was

[3] Other informants at Pyramid Lake claimed that Dick Mahwee received his powers from the ghost of a Pit River Indian, eagle, and crow. (See list of shamans and their powers given below.)

not held by lay informants at Pyramid Lake nor was it recognized by members of any of the other Paviotso groups.

As has been suggested, personal interpretation may explain this deviant concept of supernatural power. It is clear that the views quoted harmonize at least in part with the basic pattern of individualized animal and other spirits giving supernatural aid, for here in one case we find these spirits acting as messengers; they are in immediate contact with the shamans, and in the other case power from animal and other spirits is specifically mentioned.

Spirits, then, are the sources of shamanistic powers. In theory, the number of these spirits or supernatural beings is unlimited. A list of shamans and their powers was compiled in the field and checked with several informants. Although there were discrepancies in the powers ascribed to some shamans—nor is it a complete list of present-day shamans—it will illustrate the actual sources of the powers of shamans living today.

Shaman	*Source of Power*
Dick Mahwee	Eagle, crow, and the ghost of a Pit River Indian.
Abraham Mahwee	A large spotted bird which lives on the lake (unidentified), and the ghosts of three Indians, the kind of people who live far away where nobody can see them.
George Calico	Lizard and two water-babies that live in the lake.
Frank Northop	The ghost of a Pit River Indian and horse.
Judy David	Eagle.
Jack Warwick	Two horses and the ghost of a man, the same kind of power that Abraham Mahwee has (see above).
Johnny Calico	Eagle and an unidentified bird.
Pete Toby	Horse and a horse-hair rope.
Eugene Frazier	Eagle and crow.
Hattie Whitehead	Water-babies and otter.
Mary Garvey	Crow and the big mountain fly.
Julia Robinson	Eagle.
Johnny Newman	Water-babies.
Blind Bob	Claims to have power from the magpie, but has never doctored.
Paiute Harrison	Antelope and eagle.
Mary Harrison	Eagle.
Jackson Overton	Bear.
Joe Green	Otter.
Tom Mitchell[4]	Eagle, weasel, small unidentified bird living in the mountains, and another spirit unknown to the informants.
Rosie Plummer	Rattlesnake.

[4] This man is acknowledged as the most powerful shaman in recent years.

It appears that the spirit of the coyote was never a source of power, although Coyote is the most prominent character in Paviotso tales.

> Shamans never got power from Coyote. According to the old stories the Indians tell, Coyote always spoils everything. Coyote is bad. Sometimes he tries to get the soul of someone. He says, "I am going to get you and when you die, I will eat you." The coyote cannot be heard to say this, but when he has said it, it makes the victim sick. (Joe Green)
> Shamans do not get power from Coyote. Coyote causes sickness. Dogs are almost like Coyote. When a shaman doctors, dogs are kept away, otherwise he would not be successful in curing the sickness. (Rosie Plummer)

Fear of the wrath of water-babies and water-serpents noted in accounts above is not held for other spirits, save those of the elements, particularly the thunder. There seems to be no danger in ridiculing or showing lack of respect for the spirits of the animals and birds.

> The Indian doctors know the wind, clouds, and rain. A shaman talks to them. They are just like people, and they come. Anyone who makes fun of the thunder will be killed. One time a man at Schurz heard the thunder, and said, "That is nothing. I am going to fight that thunder." He went outside the house, and the thunder was heard overhead. He was hit by lightning and killed. (Tom Mitchell)

There is only one shaman who is reported to have had power from such a source. Wovoka, the prophet of the 1890 Ghost Dance, is said to have had power from two clouds.

> One was a straight high cloud. This was for snow. The other cloud was dark and close to the ground. It was for rain. Wovoka could see a man's arm sticking out of the white cloud. One time the arm would be pointing north. Another time it would be pointing south, east, or west. (Joe Green)

This statement could not be verified, but there is evidence that the leader of the 1890 Ghost Dance movement had power from several sources, including the wolf.

Another aspect of the supernatural spirits which are the source of shamanistic power is their invisibility to all but the shamans. Only the shaman can see the spirit or spirits from which he derives his power. Even when he invokes his supernatural aids at a doctoring, they are visible to him alone. Their presence is known to the others only through the shaman's account of his conversation with them. Supernatural spirits never appear to, nor are they ever heard by, anyone but those upon whom they bestow power.

Acquiring Shamanistic Power

Both men and women acquire and exercise shamanistic power. A shaman of either sex is a puhágɘm. The power possessed by either a man or a woman is likewise known by a single term, puhá. The ratio of male to female shamans, as well as the proportion of practitioners to the total population, no doubt varied considerably from generation to generation. There are at present at Pyramid Lake, in a total population of nearly five hundred, eight shamans. Three of these are women. On the Walker River Reservation, where the population is about the same, there are seven shamans, five of them women, one of whom is a Shoshoni. In past generations, female shamans do not seem to have ever outnumbered the men.

In an attempt to arrive at some idea of the total number of shamans and the ratio of men to women practitioners, I asked informants to name all who could be remembered as possessing power for curing purposes. The results at best are only approximate, but some conception of the frequency with which men and women become shamans is suggested. At Walker River several people, after a lengthy discussion among themselves, were able to name twenty shamans who were living about 1900. Of these, five were women. Three of the men were said to have been much more powerful shamans than the others. No doubt the population was somewhat greater at that time than at present, but figures are not available. Joe Green was able to name nineteen shamans living at Pyramid Lake about forty years ago. Of this number, two were women. At that time the population on this reservation was nearly seven hundred.

All informants were certain that in former years the number of shamans was considerably greater than it is today. Consequently, these estimates may serve only as a clue to the proportion of shamans, perhaps in the order of twenty to seven hundred people, at the same time giving a rough idea of how many of the shamans were women. Obviously, these ratios must have shifted from decade to decade.

In theory, female shamans may become as powerful as the male doctors. In practice, however, it appears that all the outstanding practitioners are, and have been, men. On the other hand, female shamans are highly respected and are on an equal footing with their male colleagues; some may even have stronger powers than the less prominent male shamans. Moreover, according to several informants, women can acquire powers which are used, as with men, for purposes other than curing.

> Women who have power are as strong as men shamans. One time there was a woman who had a power that protected her against bullets. When the Indians were fighting the soldiers, she rode out in front of them to attract their attention while the women and children got away. The soldiers shot at her but their bullets did not hurt her. She had the same power as men shamans. (Joe Green)

Apparently berdaches never became shamans. The several transvestites who are remembered by people living today were certainly not shamans. Lowie recorded only one case of sex-reversal among the Pyramid Lake Paviotso. This occurred some twenty years before his visit, and apparently shamanistic powers were not ascribed to the individual.[5] Sarah Winnemucca mentions the case of one cowardly warrior who was forced to don women's clothing and perform tasks allotted to that sex, but there is no reference to the possession of power.[6] This as well as the evidence in my own notes suggests that berdaches were of relatively infrequent occurrence and of slight importance. Certainly, they became shamans rarely, if ever, and clearly never as the result of their condition.

Acquiring shamanistic power, and later the exercise of power, is an individual affair. This is true both for the power derived from unsolicited dreams and from the voluntary quest. Power is never acquired by people in groups or at public performances, but is the result of private personal experiences.

The acquisition of power involves more than the development of a personal relationship with a particular spirit. When shamanistic power is conferred, the candidate not only secures a spirit helper but also acquires those special abilities or capacities neces-

[5] Lowie, *Shoshonean Ethnography*, 283.
[6] Hopkins, *Life Among the Piutes*, 70.

sary for coping with sickness; these in turn impose responsibilities and potential danger. Consequently, the possession of super-natural power signifies to the Paviotso more than is suggested by the term "guardian spirit."[7]

The central idea in the acquisition of supernatural power is dream experience. Often these dreams come unsolicited to a pro-spective shaman. In addition to these involuntary experiences, dreams may be deliberately sought in a number of places in the mountains. Supernatural power may also be inherited, but it is in dreams that the power is actually bestowed on the heir. It is, then, through the experiences in dreams, which may either be sought or may be spontaneous, that a shaman characteristically acquires his power. One shaman may say that power came to him unasked, an-other may claim to have inherited his power, and a third relates that he acquired power in a certain cave in the mountains. Still, each gained a supernatural spirit as a familiar and as a powerful ally in certain undertakings, also an exacting and cruel taskmas-ter, through the same medium. In short, all shamans gain power from a fundamentally similar experience, differing only in the way in which it is initiated.

Supernatural power is usually acquired after maturity. Children were known to have had shamanistic power, however, and even to have doctored the sick. One such case was reported at Pyramid Lake.

> I have seen boys who were about twenty or twenty-five get power and start doctoring, but a young doctor is not powerful. When a shaman gets to be sixty or seventy he knows everything. Then he is a very strong doctor. (Joe Green)

Life crises, such as puberty or the period of mourning for hus-band, wife or child, are not recognized as times when shamanistic power is to be acquired or lost. Those who seek dream-experiences in caves are always adults. Statements of informants indicate that

---

[7] Throughout this discussion, the term "power" will be used to designate not only those spirits which give supernatural aid to the shaman, but also the special restrictions and responsibilities placed on recipients of supernatural visitations. It is felt that the term "guardian spirit" implies a somewhat different relationship between an individual and his supernatural familiar. See, for example, Ruth Benedict's *The Vision in Plains Culture*, 13 f., for a statement of the relation that exists in the western Plains between an individual and the spirit that has blest him, also the same author's *The Guardian Spirit in North America*.

power may come at any time during life at the volition of the spirits or powers.

Power that comes unsolicited makes itself known through repeated dreams. The spirit which is the source of power appears repeatedly in these dreams to instruct the dreamer.

> A man dreams that a spirit of deer, eagle, or bear comes to him. The spirit tells him that he is to be a doctor. When a man first dreams this way he does not believe it. Then the dream comes again. He dreams this way for a long time. The spirit tells him to collect eagle feathers, wild tobacco, a stone pipe, a rattle, and other things. When he gets these things he becomes a doctor. He learns his songs when the spirit comes and sings to him. (Nick Downington)

The dreams, both in form and in content, conform to no rigidly fixed pattern. One person may see an animal or a ghost in his dreams; another may only hear the voice of the spirit which gives him his power. There seems, however, to be an emphasis on auditory experiences in dreams. Usually in the first dream, the prospective shaman only hears the spirit singing and talking. In later dreams the spirit is seen. This is not always the case, for some shamans had visual evidence of the presence of supernatural powers in their first, as well as in later, dream-experiences.

The instructions given the novice shaman in dreams are also varied. One may be told to follow certain rules in eating or in other daily habits; for another the details will be quite different. As was mentioned in the statements above, the dreamer is told also to collect certain objects to be used in doctoring. There is, then, a certain generalized type of dream through which power is acquired. Within this framework, the dreams of individuals are quite varied. Differences in instructions received by shamans in dreams are often given as the explanation of the variety of ways in which shamans doctor or perform their other functions. Several informants stated that no two shamans have precisely the same dreams. Consequently, there are numerous differences in detail in carrying out shamanistic practices. These differences are never ascribed to individual interpretation, but are attributed to the whims of shamans' spirits reflected in the instructions received from the supernatural helpers in dreams or at the curing performance. Moreover, individuals vary in the number of dreams that are had before shamanistic practice is undertaken. One man may dream of a spirit only a few times; then, recognizing the meaning of his experience, he will feel fully qualified to take up doctoring. Another novice shaman may dream repeatedly for a year or more before he enters upon his profession. No doubt the degree of suggestibility of various individuals is an important factor in determining the frequency of dreams. The desire of one person to become a shaman may lead to the interpretation that certain dreams have conferred power, whereas another may refuse out of fear to undertake shamanistic practice. If a person dreams of being a shaman only once, or even several times, it is not thought that he must obey the call.

It should be noted that relatively few complete dream-experiences were recorded. This is in part due to the feeling that the actual content of the dream itself was of no importance. The instructions that the dreamer received were all that mattered. Consequently, though few people related dreams in any detail, the knowledge and the instructions gained through such experiences were carefully reported by informants. There was no reluctance on the part of either shamans or laymen in discussing dream-experiences; all talked freely on this subject.

An account of the dreams by which power was given to one shaman will serve to illustrate the characteristic features of this sort of experience.

> I was getting to be a doctor. My father was a doctor, and I got to be one just the same as he. In my dream, I heard a song. It was coming from the north. It was coming just a few feet above the ground. I heard that song. I heard it just one night. The song came all night. That was all I heard the first night.
>
> In dreams after that I saw a horse coming from the east. When I first heard him, he was on the other side of the mountain. Then I saw him come over the ridge. He came toward me and when he got close, he made a big circle around me. Then he went back. That horse had nothing to do with my power.
>
> My father used to doctor. He had power from the otter. I had the same power. After I dreamed about the horse, the otter came to me in my dreams. He told me to get his skin and to cut it into a strip about four inches wide down the length of the back from the head to the top of the tail and including the eyes and ears. Then he told me to get two eagle tail-feathers and put them in two holes in the skin at the neck and

to tie them inside with buckskin. The feathers lay flat on the fur side of the skin. The otter told me to keep the skin and the eagle-feathers. He told me to use the skin and feathers when sickness is bad and hard to cure. He said, "When there is very bad sickness and no doctor can cure it, take the skin out of your sack and put it in front of you. Then you are going to try to cure." I was ready to doctor then. When I doctored, the otter gave me my songs.

This account then goes on to relate how a mistake was made in the care of the paraphernalia and, as a result, the informant lost his power. This illustrates the belief that if the exact details of the instructions given by the supernatural spirit are not followed, the offending shaman will suffer illness and loss of power.

After I got my power, I tried doctoring a few times. Then one night the otter came to me again in a dream. He told me that I should get another tail-feather of the eagle. He said, "Take a round piece of abalone shell about the size of a quarter and fasten it to the feather." It was then that I spoiled my power. I had been thinking for some time that the otter-skin was too long. It was about four feet from the head to the tip of the tail. So I cut the head off. After I had done this I got sick. The last time I dreamed about the otter was when I was sick. I felt dizzy. I did not feel very good. I saw the otter jump into the upper end of Pyramid Lake. Then I saw him running on the desert. That was the last time I saw the otter. I had to call in a powerful shaman [Tom Mitchell] to cure me. He came and doctored me. He said to me, "I found out that you cut off the otter's head. That is what made you sick. When you did that the otter went away. You will never see him again. You cut the head off and now you are just like the otter. He does not know anything, and you are the same way." I never dreamed again of the otter when I got well. If I had not cut that piece from the skin I would now be a doctor. (Joe Green)

Very often dream-experience, if not understood, will result in sickness. In this event it may be necessary to have a shaman interpret dreams and restore the dreamer to health.

A man has the same dream a number of times. Then he knows the power to be a shaman is in him. Sometimes it makes him very sick. He must do what the power tells him. One man, who is still living here [Reno], was sick about a year. He almost died. When he was sick he went into trances and his body was stiff as a board. He dreamed that he went to the land of the dead. He dreamed that way all the time when he was sick. He said that ghosts of dead people came and tried to steal his soul. His father was a shaman. The man almost died, but his father finally cured him. (Harry Sampson)

The first few dreams in which supernatural spirits appear can be safely disregarded. But shortly, if the instructions received in the dream are not followed, it is necessary to call a shaman to doctor the patient. In the course of curing, the shaman tells the patient to do as he had been told in his dreams. Then, if the summons is obeyed, recovery is assured. Usually a person is reluctant to become a shaman, and assumes his powers and follows the spirit's bidding only when he is told by other shamans that otherwise death will result. Likewise throughout the rest of the shaman's life he must follow carefully all the instructions given him by his supernatural power. If any part of shamanistic paraphernalia which has been collected at the behest of the shaman's spirit is lost or destroyed, the shaman not only loses his power, but, as has been noted, sickness also results. Death may also follow any other very serious breaches of the injunctions placed on the shaman by the spirits.

In addition to those who receive shamanistic power from involuntary dreams, there are individuals whose desire for power is sufficiently strong to cause them to undertake a voluntary quest. There are certain places, such as caves in the mountains, where power can be acquired.[8] Eight or ten such places are known today, and perhaps formerly there were still others which are now forgotten.

In some of these places, only power for certain undertakings can be sought; in others several kinds of spirit aid can be gained. The tests that are imposed upon the seeker differ also according to the place where the power is sought.

> Power is sought on a mountain near Wabusca. This power protects a man against bullets. It makes him a great warrior. When a man gets power at this place he must run down the side of the mountain without breathing. If he does not do this the power will not help him. This place is not like the other places where power is acquired. Here the noises of all the animals are not heard the way they are in the caves. Only power to be a warrior comes from this mountain. This place is called tágwan[i]. A long time ago men got power there. No one goes there nowadays.
>
> There is another place near Fallon where power is sought. The power

---

[8] Lowie recorded that, ". . . in the Walker River district there was a mountain where people went in quest of a vision." *Notes on Shoshonean Ethnography*, 294.

to be a doctor can be acquired on this mountain. Big rocks roll down when a person goes there to seek power. If one steps out of the way of these rolling rocks, the power will not come. The rocks come within a couple of feet of the person who is seeking power and then disappear. That is the way the spirits test people who go there to get power. The mountain is called wayíkudəgwa'. (Rosie Plummer)

There are no preparations for the power-quest. The man who seeks a vision does not fast either before he undertakes the quest or during his stay in the cave. Nor is the quest for power accompanied by self-torture or extended physical exertion.

Late in the afternoon, the man who seeks power goes to a cave where, he has heard, it is possible to acquire power. Food for a midnight and a morning meal may be taken along. Upon entering the cave, the aspirant for supernatural power asks for the particular kind of power that he desires. He then makes simple preparations for spending the night there. Power comes simply as a result of the aspirant's request and his concentration on the desire for power. One of the informants, Dick Mahwee, who sought and received his power in a cave, gave an account of his experiences.[9] His version will serve as a fairly representative statement of this manner of acquiring power.

> When I was a young man I had dreams in which I doctored people. I did not take those dreams seriously. My uncle was an Indian doctor. He knew what was coming to me. He told me to be careful in talking, not to speak harshly [in order not to offend the supernatural spirits]. I did not become a doctor from these dreams. Finally, I decided to go to the cave near Dayton. I was about fifty then. My uncle did not tell me to go there. I just decided to do this myself.
>
> I went into the cave in the evening. As soon as I got inside, I prayed and asked for power to doctor sickness. I said, "My people are sick. I want to save them. I want to keep them well. You can help me make them well. I want you to help me to save them. When they have died give me power to bring them back [return the lost soul]." I said this to the spirit in the cave. It is not a person. It comes along with the darkness. This is a prayer to the night.
>
> Then I tried to go to sleep. It was hard to sleep there. I heard all kinds of noises. I could hear all the animals. There were bears, mountain lions, deer, and other animals. They were all in caves in the moun-

[9] It may be of interest to note that he related his experiences in detail each summer during the three seasons in the field. These accounts recorded a year apart agreed in all details.

tain. After I went to sleep I could hear people at a doctoring. They were down at the foot of the mountain. I could hear their voices and the songs. Then I heard the patient groan. A doctor was singing and doctoring for him. A woman with a sage-brush shoot in her hand danced. She moved around the fire jumping at every step. Each time she jumped she said, "hə', hə', hə'." Then the shaman sprinkled water on the patient with sage-brush. The singing and dancing went on for a long time. Then the singing stopped. The patient had died and the people began to cry.

After a while the rock where I was sleeping began to crack like breaking ice. A man appeared in the crack. He was tall and thin. He had the tail-feather of an eagle in his hand. He said to me, "You are here. You have said the right words. You must do as I tell you. Do that or you will have a hard time. When you doctor, you must follow the instructions that the animals give you. They will tell you how to cure the sickness. I have this feather in my hand. You must get feathers like it. You are also to find the things that go with it. Get dark beads. Put them on the quills of the feathers and tie a strip of buckskin to the quills. Also get a hoof of a deer, and down from the eagle. With these you can go to people to cure them. These are your weapons against sickness. You must get three rolls of tobacco. You can use them to tell your patients what made them sick and then you can cure them. The tobacco will also help you if you are choked with clots of saliva when you suck out the disease. With this you are beginning to be a doctor. You will get your songs when you doctor. The songs are now in a straight line [ready for use]. Bathe in the water at the foot of the cliff and paint yourself with i·bi [white paint]."

Then I woke up. It was daylight. I looked around but I could not see anyone. The man was gone and there was no sign of the animals or the people who had been singing and doctoring. Then I did as the spirit had ordered and waited to become a doctor. In about six years I had received enough instructions to begin to cure.

The success of the power-quest is dependent upon the seeker's undeviating adherence to the traditionally recognized form of procedure. If he does not go to the right place or if he refuses to stay in the cave the entire night, failure will attend his efforts. Also, as in unsolicited dreams, the instructions of the spirits must be carefully followed. Consequently, only those who do not abide by these conditions fail in the quest for power. Several informants related anecdotes of men who were unable to acquire power owing to their failure to follow the correct procedure in the quest.

Happy Dave heard about the cave where power is acquired. He went there, but he did not want to go inside the cave. He tied his horse above the cave and made his bed outside. A lizard came to Dave. It ran up one arm and down the other and then up one leg and down the other. Then it went back on the rock. After the lizard went away the wind came up. It blew very hard. Happy Dave heard the owl down by the river. He could hear the owl in spite of the wind. Later the owl came up from the river and talked to Happy Dave. The owl told him that he had not done the right thing and that he was wasting his time. He told Happy Dave that he should go home. He was to go down to the river and bathe and put i·bi [white paint] on the horse. This was to purify both the man and the horse [to prevent the sickness that would result from his improper conduct in relation with supernatural spirits]. Happy Dave told me about his experiences. It happened a long time ago. He is now dead. He never got to be a doctor. (Dick Mahwee)

With some, shamanistic power is inherited from parents or other relatives. This is not to be regarded, however, as inheritance of property in the usual sense of the term. The shaman's outfit, like other personal property at the death of the owner, is invariably destroyed. Commonly the Paviotso manifest a very strong fear of the evil consequences that would surely overtake anyone who retained personal property of the dead. The heir of shamanistic power must have that power bestowed on him in dream-experiences precisely as would any other shaman. Inheritance here is simply a strong tendency on the part of one of the children, or other relatives, of a shaman to acquire power from the same source some time after the shaman's death.

In some cases, the ghost of the deceased shaman appears in the first dream of the heir. In later dreams, the supernatural spirit that actually bestows the power appears and the ghost is no longer seen. This is not always the procedure in inheritance of power however, for the ghost of the dead relative may never appear in the prospective shaman's dreams; only the spirit which confers power comes at these times. The following statements by informants indicate the rôle of inheritance in the acquisition of supernatural power.

Power can be inherited by the son or daughter of a shaman. A son or daughter usually receives the power after a shaman dies, but sometimes a young man or woman may start to doctor while the parent is still alive. When the dreams come to the heir, he must take the power or he will be sick. When a shaman has several children, the power decides which will be a doctor. It may be the son or it may be the daughter

The eldest son does not always get the power. There is no rule, because the power always decides who is to be a shaman. Several doctors here [Pyramid Lake] inherited their powers. One woman has her father's power. She is as strong a doctor as he was. (Dick Mahwee)

In the old days, a shaman before his death did not give away his power. A son or daughter got the power after the shaman died. A few years ago a woman at Walker Lake gave her power to her daughter before she died. I do not think this was done in the old days. (Rosie Plummer)

My father had power from the otter. After he died, I dreamed about the otter and his songs. I never saw my father in my dreams. He did not decide that I would get his power. The otter decided that. Sometimes a shaman can tell before his death which child will inherit the power. One child will talk in his sleep and try to sing. The songs are not plain enough to be understood. Then the doctor knows that the child will have his power after he dies.

When my father was dying, he wanted to give me his doctoring outfit. But I knew about the danger and I did not take it. I knew it would make me sick. If I had taken his outfit he would have wanted his rattle and eagle-feather with him. He [his ghost] would come back to get these things. Then I would have got sick and died. (Joe Green)

Cases of shamanistic power being transmitted to a child while the parent is still alive are also known. In this event, both parent and child are regarded as practising shamans.

Sometimes a man will get his power from his father who is a doctor. Both can doctor at the same time. The father will tell the son how to doctor. When a boy starts going into trances, his father knows that some day his son will be a doctor. A woman can inherit power the same way. (Annie Dick)

One informant, Rosie Plummer, inherited her power from her father. He in turn had been the heir to his brother's power. Her account gives the typical beliefs for this way of acquiring shamanistic power.

When my uncle was dying, he told my father to take his power. He wanted my father to have the power to doctor. He told my father to dream about the power and get instructions for doctoring that way. The next day my uncle died. Soon after that my father began to have dreams. My uncle would appear in these dreams. He came every night in dreams. Each time he came a different way. My father did not like the dreams. He was afraid that his brother was trying to get him away [so he would die]. My uncle, before he died, had given my father a little piece of lead with a hole in the center. The hole was filled with eagle down. My father buried the lead and the eagle down. Then his brother's ghost did not bother him again. That lead and the feathers represented my uncle's power. After that my father became a powerful shaman. His power told him to catch rattlesnakes. They did not bite him. He was told to put sage-brush in his nostrils so the snakes would not hurt him.

Rattlesnake was my uncle's power; then my father had rattlesnake for his power. Now the snake gives me power. Rattlesnake came to my father in dreams. That is how he learned to treat snake-bites. Rattlesnake told him to catch rattlesnakes and take two fangs from each. He was to do this until he had ten fangs. Then he was told to take ten stone beads that were colored like rattlesnake eyes. He strung the beads and the fangs together. He used this string of beads to treat rattle-snake bites. He could also cure people who were sick.

Sometimes my father caught rattlesnakes and put them around his waist. He used to ride home carrying rattlesnakes that way. One time he put a rattlesnake on me. He told me not to move. The snake crawled all over me, but it did not bite. He had rattlesnakes with him all the time.

My father died about twenty years ago. Nearly fifteen years later, when I was about fifty, my father began to come to me in dreams. He brought his power to me. He told me to doctor. I dreamed about him three or four times before I believed that I would doctor. After a while the power started to come to me when I dreamed. Then I stopped dreaming about my father. The rattlesnake told me what to do. The snake helps me doctor now. It comes to me when I dream. Several times it has told me to catch snakes, but I have not done it. This has not yet made me sick.

It is difficult to state what proportion of shamans at any one time have inherited powers. Nearly everyone has or had either close or distant kin with shamanistic power. There seems to be a general feeling that at least one child of a shaman will inherit powers. On the other hand, there is good evidence that in many cases a shaman's powers are lost at death. It also seems evident that inheritance here is but a variation on the theme of acquiring power through dream-experience.

Related to the practice of transferring power before death to the son or daughter is the idea that it can be shared with another. However, when a shaman gives his power to some member of his family, usually that person has already been set apart from others as having a predisposition to acquire power. This is exhibited early in life by dreams and by talking while asleep. Transfer in this fashion appears to happen frequently, for it was described by a number of informants who knew of several shamans who had acquired power from a parent during the lifetime of that individual. On the other hand, sharing power with any person not so disposed is not a common practice. Only one incident of transferring power in return for property or other considerations was recorded.

There are, then, three general ways in which the Paviotso may acquire power, but all depend fundamentally upon the same type of experience. In spite of the many opportunities thus afforded for acquiring power, it is evident that relatively few people actually become shamans. The explanation doubtless is to be found in the danger involved in both the acquisition and the use of supernatural power.

Another point that emerges from these accounts is the extreme simplicity of the voluntary power-quest. Essentially, it is little more than the deliberate seeking for the usual dream-experiences accompanied by rather simple tests of the candidate's courage. The long and arduous physical exertions that characterize the Plateau quest and the fasting and self-torture of the search for power on the western Plains are totally unknown to the Paviotso. It is as though the deliberate quest for power here were lightly superimposed upon an older basic pattern in which shamanistic power was derived from dream-experiences alone.

Loss of Power

A shaman is never secure at any time in the possession of his power. Careless treatment of paraphernalia or the flouting of instructions given by the spirits may deprive the shaman of his ability to cure disease. Moreover, careless or malicious acts of others may endanger the shaman's power. If a spectator at a curing ceremony does not carry out the precise requests of the practitioner in handling food, painting the face or body, maintaining silence at specified times during the performance, or other special forms of behavior demanded of those present, harm in the form of failure to effect a cure as well as sickness for the shaman is likely to follow. Frequent instances of illness and loss of power among shamans were attributed by informants to these or similar missteps or to abuses in utilizing the special powers conferred upon these people.

Power, then, is not benign. When power is acquired, the shaman suffers, and throughout his life he is constantly threatened not only with sickness but with death as well. He is endangered not only by his own acts, but also by either deliberate or thoughtless behavior of others. The shaman, like anybody else, as we shall see later, may become ill as the result of some involuntary act, either of his own or of others.

PARAPHERNALIA

The versions of dreams that have been given contain some indication of the variety of objects with which a shaman must equip himself. A typical kit that is gathered at the behest of the shaman's power contains a rattle (wisábaya), the tail-feathers of the eagle, magpie, or some other bird, down from the same bird, stone, shell, or bone beads, a tubular pipe, wild tobacco, often a peculiarly-shaped stone, and the large hollow wing- or leg-bone of the duck or pelican. The variation in equipment is attributed to the differences in instructions given shamans in the course of their dream-experiences. Some parts of the paraphernalia, however, are standard equipment and are to be found in the possession of all shamans. These include the pipe, tobacco, rattle, beads, feathers and down.[10]

The paraphernalia is kept in a bag made of badger's skin. When the skin of the badger is not available, otter- or weasel-fur, or a piece of buckskin, will serve equally well. This bag or sack is a crude affair. The edges of the untanned skin are simply sewn together, leaving an opening which is not fastened. It is called puhámakɔ^{gwai}odúna. Several informants stated that each part of the paraphernalia is wrapped separately before placing it in the container; probably this practice varies from one shaman to another. The shaman always keeps his paraphernalia with him. At night it is placed under his pillow, nowadays under the bed. As has been noted, the loss of the kit or any part of the contents results in sickness for the shaman.

There are two kinds of shaman's rattles. One is the jingling deer hooflet type; the other has a drum of dried skin of deer's ears. The

[10] Lowie, *Shoshonean Ethnography*, 294, notes that shamans' paraphernalia differ, that some use an eagle-tail, whereas others have a magpie feather and that they use a rattle.

second type is made by scraping the skin clean of hair, soaking it in water, and sewing together the edges. Sand is packed inside, and the skin is allowed to dry until it is hard and stiff. Then the sand is removed and a handle of greasewood or willow about eight inches long is put through holes made in the center of the two pieces of skin. The handle projects an inch or a little less on one side of the rattle. It is fastened in place firmly with sinew. Small pebbles, usually gathered on an ant-hill, are put into the drum, and the opening is closed. Nowadays, circular pieces of deerskin frequently take the place of the skin from the ears. A variation in this rattle is produced by fastening two containers of pebbles together at one end of the handle, making a double-headed rattle.

The other type, the deer-claw rattle, is similar to the rattle used in girls' adolescence rites by a number of tribes in northern California. Anywhere from fifteen or twenty to fifty or even more deer-claws are used, depending upon the number available. A hole is made in the tip of each hooflet and a short piece of buckskin thong knotted at one end is put through the hole from the inside. The hooflet is then fastened by the thong to a willow or greasewood handle. The knot inside the hooflet prevents the buckskin from pulling through the hole. The claws dangle in a bunch an inch or two from the handle, which is usually eight or ten inches long.

Both types of rattles are known as wisábaya. The choice of the type of rattle to be used by each shaman is dictated by his power.

The tail-feather contained in the shaman's paraphernalia has a piece of buckskin thong about ten inches long tied to the quill. Down is also fastened to the thong and one or two beads of bone, shell or stone are strung on it close to the feathers. When the shaman doctors, the tail-feathers, together with the down and the beads, are fastened by the buckskin to a dressed willow stick three or four feet long. The pointed end of this stick (puhátumadápuipi) is placed in the ground beside the patient's head. The stick may be painted with red or white bands. The design of the painting is revealed to the shaman by his power. A fresh stick is used each time a shaman cures. The particular kind of feathers used by the shaman does not indicate his source of power. A shaman might have power from an animal and keep an eagle-feather in his outfit. In fact, eagle-feathers are employed more frequently than those from any other bird.

Because they are used by nearly all shamans, eagle-feathers are much in demand. Eagles were formerly captured, especially when young, and kept in cages. After the tail-feathers had been plucked several times, the eagle was released; they were never killed. Some informants said that this was because these birds were considered almost sacred, as their feathers played such an important rôle in doctoring. Nests from which eagles were captured were claimed as private property, and were inherited along with land-rights as a family possession.

The shaman's pipe (tóic) has a tubular bowl with a wooden stem. Nowadays, however, cigarettes frequently take the place of the pipe and tobacco in shamanistic performances. Consequently, few shamans have pipes. Shamans might also use their pipes for social smoking, passing them around among companions. The shaman's pipe differed in no details from those employed for secular purposes. Both the pipe used in curing and the one used for pleasure are designated by the same term (tóic).

The tobacco (puibámo) is the local wild variety which is smoked both for pleasure and for curing purposes. A shaman usually gathers and dries his tobacco in a secret place far from camp, in order to escape the danger of using tobacco that has been in the presence of menstruating women. It is believed that if a woman in that condition were to touch, or even be near, the tobacco, the shaman's efficacy in curing would be endangered. Similar precautions are also taken with tobacco that is smoked for pleasure. The prepared tobacco is kept in a small sack which is carried in the larger bag with the rest of the paraphernalia. When doctoring, shamans also smoke the various mixtures of tobacco, leaves, and grasses used on social occasions.

In addition to the standard paraphernalia, shamans also have in their outfits other equipment required by their powers, such as bone whistles. The whistles are made from the wing-bones of eagles and other large birds and are four to six inches long. It is a simple hollow tube, without holes, held against the chin with one end at the lower lip. The breath is blown across this end. These instruments are used by some shamans at the beginning of the curing performance in order to call the powers. They are little used today, however, and it is doubtful that they were formerly commonly included with the paraphernalia. It was reported that a shaman uses a whistle only if told to do so by his power. When the whistle is not in use, it is stuffed with feathers.

A bone or wooden tube six to twelve inches in length, used in sucking out the disease, might also be included in the outfit if required by a shaman's spirit. When not in use, such a tube is filled with feathers. Commonly the shaman sucks the cause of disease from the patient by applying his mouth to the part of the body where, according to the diagnosis, the pain is localized. Some shamans, however, suck the disease from the patient through these tubes.

Paraphernalia in excess of the common standard equipment does not give a shaman stronger or even special powers. Nevertheless, unique or unusual additions are not looked upon as nonessential elaborations of the shaman's equipment. Everything in the kit is important and has a meaning, for if only a single feather is missing, the shaman faces sickness and supernatural impotence. All paraphernalia must be carefully preserved and used only in accordance with the instructions received by the shaman in his dreams. When power is secured from several sources, say from several species of birds and animals, each spirit is represented in the shaman's paraphernalia. If part of the outfit is lost or disposed of, the particular power thus offended will cause the shaman to be sick, but he will be deprived of only that part of his power bestowed by the outraged spirit. The shaman may not lose all of his powers through the anger of a single spirit. It is reported that Abraham Mahwee, a shaman at Pyramid Lake, formerly had power from the bear in addition to the powers ascribed to him today. Grieving over the death of his wife a number of years ago, he threw away that part of his paraphernalia which had been collected at the command of the bear. Soon after, he became seriously ill and had to call in another shaman to doctor him. Since his recovery, he has not been able to get the bear to help him in doctoring, although he has not lost the powers given him by other spirits.

CAUSE OF DISEASE

The Paviotso attribute disease to supernatural agencies. Minor ailments, however, are recognized and cured by "home remedies." The knowledge of these treatments is even today widespread and is by no means restricted to the professional equipment of the shaman. Therefore, only illness which results from supernatural causes and which requires the exercise of the shaman's power to bring about recovery will be considered here. Many informants made a strong contrast between sickness today and formerly. It is said that before the whites came, the diseases of the present time were not known; that the Indians suffered only from aches and pains which were caused by sorcery, by dreams, or other supernatural causes.

Two concepts of the cause of disease widespread in the primitive world are current among the Paviotso. It is believed that sickness results from the intrusion of a pathogenic tangible object, or again, an individual may die as a result of the loss of his soul.[11] Shamans may also suffer from the breach of tabu, that is, as the result of breaking any of the restrictions which are placed upon them by their powers. Yet these three categories of the causes of disease are somewhat artificial, as the Paviotso do not clearly distinguish among them. According to their notions, sickness results from a dream, and in such cases a shaman may at one time suck out an intrusive object to bring about a cure, whereas on another occasion it may be necessary to return the lost soul of the patient. Again from the point of view of the Paviotso, sorcerers can cause sickness; but here too, both soul loss and intrusive objects are involved. Therefore, it would seem from the point of view of native belief that a more realistic classification of the causes of disease would take into consideration sickness caused by such agents as

[11] Lowie, *Shoshonean Ethnography*, 294–295, observes that shamans return the lost soul of patients. Clements, *Primitive Concepts of Disease*, Table I, 194, implies the absence of this belief among the Paviotso. His reference to "disease object intrusion" in Lowie's account (292) applies specifically to the Ute at Ignacio and Navaho Springs, not, as is cited, to the Paviotso. Clements's citation for the concept of soul loss among the Ute on the basis of Lowie's statement on p. 294 is likewise erroneous, as Lowie mentions this belief only for the Paviotso. It seems that in using Lowie's material to determine the distribution of disease concepts in the Great Basin, Clements inferred that if a belief is recorded for the Ute it must exist among the Paviotso and vice versa.

sorcery, dreams, ghosts, and animals, as well as the illness of shamans resulting from mistakes or disobedience either of the practitioner or of others.

Dreams (nɔsi) are commonly the cause of sickness. That is, the
dream itself is directly responsible, not prophetic of, illness. The
experiences in such dreams usually are connected with ghosts of
the dead or visions of sickness and death. Often the dreamer will
not suffer the ill effects of his dream, but a relative or a member of
the household is the victim of the illness so caused. These disease-
causing dreams seem to be entirely involuntary; one dreams—with
no conscious desire to cause harm—that another is, or will be, ill;
and shortly thereafter that individual becomes sick. Thus, illness
among children is commonly believed to result from the dreams of
parents. A father will dream that his child is ill; a few days later
the child is stricken and a shaman must be called in. If the shaman
is not called very soon after the first manifestation of the sickness,
the child will die. Visitors, as well as the parents, may bring about
the illness of children as the result of dreams. In the summer of
1934, one such incident caused some excitement on the Pyramid
Lake Reservation. As several informants reconstructed the affair,
the following incidents led to a threat of murder.

> Joe Overall was visiting Rawhide Henry. After they ate at noon, Joe
> fell asleep at the table. When he woke up he said that he had dreamed
> about Rawhide's grandchild. He said that in the dream the girl was sick
> and weak. She was very sick. She was almost dead. The girl's parents
> told Joe to do something to take away the dream. Otherwise it looked
> bad for the girl. The girl's mother asked Joe to wash the girl and pray
> so the dream would go away. He did not want to do it. He told them
> that she would be all right. In a few hours the girl was sick. They called
> in a shaman to doctor the girl. The next day Rawhide's family wanted
> to kill Joe. Joe was a shaman a long time ago, but he lost his power.
> They think that he may have a little power left and that he used it to
> make the girl sick.

The contents of the dreams which result in sickness are varied.
A relative may be seen to be ill or dying; voices may speak of sickness, or the dreamer may experience aches and pains. Apparently,
in these dreams spirits or ghosts are not seen.

> Dreams about sickness just come natural. There do not seem to be
> any spirits that cause them. The dream just comes and then soon after
> you are sick. (Nick Downington)

People are often sick from dreams. The sickness comes in different ways. One person might see himself sick in his dream. Another person dreams that he sees a shaman coming toward him, or a voice may be heard telling the dreamer to do certain things.Other people dream that a shaman tries to touch them or to give them something. These dreams are bad and make people sick. (Rosie Plummer)

As has been noted, illness may also result from seeing or having other experiences in dreams with a ghost (sa'ab°), either that of a friend, relative, or of a stranger. These dreams also are said to be involuntary. This type of dream-experience is greatly feared as a source of disease. Probably the Paviotso regard dreams as the chief cause of all illness.

In some instances, it may be possible to prevent sickness if the bad effects of the dream can be counteracted before the malady has seriously affected the victim. Upon awakening, if the dream is recalled, the sleeper addresses a prayer to the sun in order to pre-vent illness. Early in the morning, just as the sun is coming up, the dreamer asks the sun for good health. A typical prayer of this kind is: "Take my bad dream with you. Take away my pains as you go down in the evening. Take them and throw them into the cool water down below." Very often, however, the dreams are not remembered, and sickness results. Only a shaman can then over-come the evil influences of the dream and bring about recovery. The shaman finds in the curing performance that a dream brought on the illness. Then the one who had experienced the dream is forced to recall its content and the time that it occurred. This pub-lic confession of the dream is a necessary part of the cure. Until the dreamer admits to the shaman the experiences that caused the sickness, further efforts to bring about a cure are ineffectual.

Ghosts are greatly feared as a source of evil, especially as they cause illness. These dreaded spirits are the souls of dead people. Even among the living, the soul wanders in dreams from its place in the body. The seat of the soul is placed by some in the head and by others in the chest. The soul or spirit is designated by either the term sóyəp, or numəmugu'ª.[12] Frequently these terms are ren-

---

[12] This is the term that Lowie recorded for the spirit or soul among the Paviotso, *Shoshonean Ethnography*, 294, 296. It occurs among the Wind River, Lemhi, and Seed Eater Shoshone in practically the same form. Lowie, *The Northern Shoshone*, 226; Hoebel, *Shoshone Religion*, ms.

dered in English by interpreters as "the mind." Also in speaking of the loss of the soul, such expressions as "he lost his mind" or "his mind was gone" are employed. It is believed that when breathing stops, the soul leaves the body. Instead of departing at once for the land of the dead, the souls of the dead may turn into ghosts (sa'ab°) and plague the living. The ghost's intentions, however, may not be malicious. It is thought that one may linger near the camp in order to take along the soul of some member of the family of the dead person for company on the journey to the land of the dead. It is said that other ghosts, especially "those of people who were mean during life," may be intentionally malignant. These ghosts often assume the form of animals, especially coyotes, and in such forms appear to the living and cause illness. It is therefore evident that ghosts seen either when awake or in dreams are causes of illness.

It is not thought dangerous for shamans to see or communicate with ghosts. It is said that their powers give them immunity from possible harmful consequences of this contact. The appearance of a ghost to one who is not a shaman is certain to cause immediate and serious illness, unless precautions are taken to counteract their contaminating influence. For example, when a whirlwind in which ghosts travel is seen, dirt is thrown in its direction and it is driven away with these words: "Stay away from me. You are no good. I can see you. I know what you are. You go the other way." However, even this formula will not always succeed in preventing the sickness that frequently follows such an experience. The danger of sickness from ghosts seen in dreams can often be forestalled by prayers directed to the sun as it comes up in the morning.

Sickness caused by ghosts may, in part, be related to the loss of the soul, for, as has been stated, some ghosts attempt to steal souls from the living in order to have the company of loved ones on the journey to the land of the dead. However, all cases of illness resulting from the visits of ghosts are not of this order. Many suffering from such experiences are cured, not by the return of the soul, but by following the instructions which the shaman receives from his powers when he goes into a trance to diagnose the case. Moreover, soul loss is not entirely due to the kidnaping by ghosts of souls of the living. Several people are reported to have had their souls restored by shamans when they were thought to have died. In these cases, it is claimed that the soul has strayed, in which case it must be found by the shaman and returned. Another explanation frequently given is that souls start for the land of the dead and that they either loiter along the way or are refused admission at the entrance to the afterworld, where they are told that they are not yet ready to join the dead. In either event, the shaman has the opportunity to find the soul and attempt to induce it to return. The following statement is a generally accepted view of this point.

> When anyone dies his soul goes up. All we know about this is what shamans tell. They learn about the way the souls go when they bring back the dead [restore the soul]. After death, a soul stays near the body for a little while. When someone dies suddenly, there is time to get a shaman. If the soul has not gone far, he can bring it back. He goes into a trance to bring back the soul. When the soul has gone a long way to the afterworld, the shaman cannot do anything. It has too much of a start to the land of the dead and he cannot overtake it. (Rosie Plummer)

It is thought that the soul often leaves the body during sleep. When this happens, serious harm will result if the sleeper is suddenly awakened. Shamans are especially subject to this danger. Accordingly, a sleeping shaman is not disturbed.

> When anyone dreams, his spirit or soul wanders away. It is dangerous to awaken a person suddenly. His soul may be away doing something. It may be far away. If the person is suddenly awakened, his soul does not get back. He will lose his mind. He will get sick and if a shaman does not doctor very soon, he will die.
> When a shaman is asleep, no one is supposed to wake him. If he is awakened, it makes his powers angry. The shaman will lose his mind. Even today, people believe that it is dangerous to go near a sleeping shaman. They might make a noise and awaken him suddenly. Then his powers would take away his mind. (Rosie Plummer)

Other sources of illness, such as that resulting from the acquisition of power, from the loss of paraphernalia, or from carelessness at a doctoring, have been noted in the accounts of other phases of shamanism discussed above. Certain dreams regarded elsewhere as harmful, such as the dreams of blood, are not feared by the Paviotso.

It is believed that animals as well as ghosts can bring sickness to man. Apparently, such sickness may result from a deliberate malicious effort as in the case of the coyote; with other animals it may be involuntary or the means of punishment.

> Once a man dreamed that three coyotes came to him. They said, "Tell us who is a good man. We will get him and eat him. If you do not tell us, we will come and eat you." The man believed them, so he told them about a woman. A few days after the man had this dream, the woman was sick. They got a shaman to doctor her. He sang for two nights before he knew what made her sick. Then he saw three coyotes in a cloud. Only the heads could be seen. He saw that they were coming to get the woman. He told the woman's family what the coyote had done. They were coming then. When they came close and saw the shaman, they were afraid. They went away and never bothered the woman again. The shaman told her to put red paint on all her joints. She was to paint red and white bands around her joints. [Treatment in this fashion is customary in curing illness caused by dreams.] Coyote could see that paint when he was a long way off. He did not like it so he never came again. (Joe Green)

Other game animals, especially large game, such as antelope and mountain sheep, can also cause illness. The owl appears, prophetically perhaps, in dreams to bring sickness. Gophers, too are thought to be a sign of sickness and death, but it is doubtful that they cause either. When gophers are caught, they are skinned and the skin is spread over the belly of the carcass. Both are then hung up on the south side of a bush, tree, or house. Gophers may also be burned until only ashes remain. In the course of either operation, a prayer in some such words as these is recited: "You tried to give me bad luck. Now you will be destroyed."

Sorcery is an extremely potent source of illness. The sorcerer secures his power from the same sources and in the same way as the shaman who practices for the general good. In fact, to the Paviotso a sorcerer is a shaman who utilizes his power not in the socially accepted way but in a dangerous and anti-social fashion; he has corrupted potentially beneficial power in such a way as to cause harm. The sorcerer is frequently designated by the term for shaman, puhágəm. There is, however, another word for the sorcerer, numótukód° (eater of people), but the former seems to be more commonly used.

The sorcerer recites no incantations, nor does he work spells, to overcome his victims. Cast-off clothing, nail-parings, hair-combings, and the images of intended victims, are not used by the sorcerer in causing sickness and death. In fact, none of the techniques usually associated with the practice of either sympathetic or contagious magic is to be found among the Paviotso. Frequently the sorcerer achieves his end simply by concentrating his thoughts on the desired end, the wish for the destruction of the victim by sickness. A sorcerer may also cause illness by touching a person, by handing him food, or giving him a pipe to smoke. The sorcerer does not allow even his victim to become aware of the effort being made to harm him. Discovery of the sorcerer's practices comes only when a shaman is successful in diagnosing the malady of the victim. It is said that sorcerers can cause people either to die suddenly or to suffer a lingering illness.

Often, when sickness results from sorcery, a tangible substance enters the victim's body. That is, in the current categories of such concepts, the sorcerer brings about "disease-object intrusion." These objects are variously described as a small stone, a little black lizard, a worm, insects, a sliver of obsidian, and miniature figures of men, animals, or birds. None of these is thought to have been "shot" into the victim; nor are such objects used in any way to bring about sickness. In the words of one informant, "The sorcerer thinks about a lizard and that is what causes sickness." The sorcerer then simply concentrates on something, and with the assistance of his power it, or its miniature, is injected by some supernatural process into the victim and sickness results. The disease-object must be sucked out in order to bring about the victim's recovery.

Sorcerers appear never to practice their art for material gain or at the request of another. Securing the services of a sorcerer by means of persuasion or bribery to wreak vengeance on an enemy is totally foreign to Paviotso thinking. The sorcerer works in secret entirely for his own ends. At least this is true when he first uses his power for evil purposes. Later, after he has caused the illness and death of a number of people, he is powerless to withstand the impulse to kill. Then his activities become completely involuntary and he is unable to restrain his lust for murder.

After a shaman poisons one person, he cannot stop. When the first victim is dead, he tries to poison others. Then he always wants to make people sick and kill them. (Joe Green)

If he has sufficient power, a shaman who has been the victim of a sorcerer may extract the cause of disease and without the aid of another practitioner cast off the ill effects of his enemy's magic.

As sorcerers are believed to cause so much of the illness afflicting the Paviotso, they are greatly feared. Anyone suspected of sorcery is treated with every respect and consideration in order not to arouse his wrath and ill-will. It is said that any request or demand made by a known sorcerer is never refused out of fear of the revenge that might be taken through witchcraft. Those who fear a particular shaman will, if possible, avoid accepting anything from him or touching his person.

In aboriginal times, sorcerers were put to death when detected in frequent killings. Their guilt was established then as now, by shamans who determined not only the nature of sickness but also the person responsible. An accusation of this sort by a shaman of standing was probably tantamount to conviction. When a sorcerer claimed several victims, the entire group became concerned and demanded the death of the guilty person. The execution was carried out by several men appointed for the task, or a large number of people fell upon the sorcerer and killed him. The usual practice was to burn the house over the murdered sorcerer; otherwise the body was buried in the usual manner.

If a sorcerer had not become notorious, members of a victim's family might take it upon themselves to avenge the death of a relative. The sorcerer, known to them from the shaman's diagnosis, was stabbed, clubbed, or shot. As in the communal execution, the house was burned with the corpse inside. As far as can be learned, the sorcerer's family rarely attempted retaliation for these murders. In so far as pre-Caucasian conditions can be determined from the memories of living people, it can safely be said that the fear of sorcery was easily the chief source of intra-tribal strife and violence; that the charge of witchcraft more frequently than anything else led to the killing of one Paviotso by another. Suspicion of sorcery is in itself sufficient to endanger social relations and even life.

It should be noted that one informant expressed the belief that all shamans who derive powers from the bear practise sorcery. According to this man, Henry Williams:

> A witch-doctor gets power from a bear. When a person is sick and dreams about a bear or about a man who looks like a bear, he knows that a doctor with that power made him sick. The power from the bear is the strongest of all the powers. A good doctor cannot cure anyone who has been bewitched by a man with bear-power.

This view was only partially confirmed by several informants. Others held that supernatural power derived from the bear carries no more possibility of sorcery than the powers of other spirits.

Shamanistic Doctoring

Curing is the chief function of the Paviotso shaman. It is always a public performance, with spectators participating to a certain extent in the treatment of the sick. These curing practices are the most important ceremonial performances of the shamans. The charming of antelope in the course of communal drives is the only other important public ceremony.[13] The Paviotso shaman gives no mid-winter ceremony to prove or strengthen his power, nor is power acquired in a public performance. Curing, then, is not merely the shamanistic treatment of disease but also an important public ceremony, without doubt the principal religious activity.

There are no public initiations or trials for the new Paviotso shamans. When a shaman feels that he has sufficient power and knowledge to undertake the treatment of patients, he lets it be known. Novices or shamans with newly acquired power usually receive no instruction from older practitioners, the knowledge revealed to them by their powers being sufficient to enable them to cure. Naturally, the shaman is already quite familiar with curing practices from attending the performances of other shamans. However, some of the younger shamans are known to have received training from older doctors, and fathers are said to have

---

[13] The dances held in connection with the Ghost Dance movements of 1870 and 1890 were not shamanistic performances. There is evidence that the prophets of both movements, with the possible exception of Wovoka, were not shamans (doctors) until after they had ceased to lead dances to bring about the return of the dead. In the minds of the Paviotso, there is no connection between those dances and the shaman's performance.

instructed sons and daughters in curing practices. It is reported that in some instances when a shaman is invited to treat his first patient, he may ask an older experienced man to help him the first night. The instructor initiates the curing and carries it on for nearly half the night. The younger shaman then takes over the performance and goes on unaided. This is entirely a personal affair between shamans, as there are no organizations or societies of shamans. Usually, instead of mutual interests and aims bringing shamans together, rivalry and jealousy, manifested by attempts to poison one another, are typical of their feelings and behavior.

In curing, each shaman is thought to derive his particular procedure from the supernatural power which directs his efforts. Therefore it seems perfectly consistent to the Paviotso that no two shamans will go through the curing performance in precisely the same way. There is, nevertheless, a general form of procedure followed by all shamans when they treat the sick. The characteristic features of this prevailing plan will first be described.

Curing always takes place at the home of the patient. In winter the mat-covered, dome-shaped house is the scene of the performance; in warm weather the shaman usually performs in the circular brush wind-break which serves as shelter while the family is away from winter quarters. Beyond sweeping the floor, nothing is done to the house in preparation for the arrival of the shaman and spectators.

The family of the sick person decides which shaman is to be called in to doctor. This decision may be made by the patient, if he is able to make his desires known. When the illness is quite serious, a shaman known to have unusually strong powers may be asked to doctor. Shamans of renown may be called in from another band, especially in serious cases, or after the failure of a local practitioner.

Shamanistic curing performances are attended by all who are living conveniently near. No public announcement is made when a shaman is about to cure, but the news of the coming event nevertheless circulates quickly. Often when a shaman is invited in the morning, everyone within walking distance has heard of the coming performance by nightfall. Consequently, a crowd never fails to gather for the curing rites.

The shamanistic performance is probably best looked upon as a blend of the social and the religious. All who attend participate, at least in a small way, by singing, which is thought to be a powerful aid in establishing contact through the shaman with the supernatural forces. This in turn assists the shaman in gaining control over malignant forces. When Paviotso shamanism was in full swing, these performances, held in a small closely packed house, must have been exciting and impressive. The singing and the shaman's tricks appear to have excited the spectators to a high emotional pitch which was followed by a relaxation of tension attended often by a general feeling of satisfaction when control of the sickness was demonstrated by the return of the soul or the extraction of a disease-object. The social aspect of these gatherings was and is today an important motive for attending. There were occasions during the night for talk and gossip, an opportunity never spurned by the Paviotso. The food provided by the patient's family at midnight also held a strong social appeal, for the religious tensions were largely relaxed for the moment. Finally, in the absence of other important religious ceremonies, these rites were charged with more feeling and emotion than any other type of community gathering.

At the present time, there is little specialization among shamans. In aboriginal times, however, certain types of disorders were treated by shamans known for their ability along special lines. Shamans with power from the rattlesnake were believed to have the greatest power for treating people bitten by that snake. Again, only shamans who derived power from water-babies could treat sickness caused by these beings. Shamans who secured their powers from ghosts specialized in curing those whose illness resulted from experiences with the souls of the dead. Still other forms of specialization in curing seem to depend on the strength of the shaman's power rather than upon its source. Some powerful shamans are believed to be especially efficacious in curing the ill-effects of dreams; others are famous for success in doctoring wounds. On the Pyramid Lake Reservation at the present time, one shaman is well known for assisting women in cases of difficult labor, not because of any particular kind of power, but because of a number of successful cures. As with this man, the renown of shamans as specialists is based entirely on success in treating certain types of afflictions. In still another form of illness, soul loss, cures can be made only by shamans who have unusually strong power. Lost souls are restored not by virtue of power from a particular source, but rather by the aid of spirits far stronger than those possessed by the ordinary shamans.

The curing performance usually takes place at night. In case of a wound, a snake-bite, or very serious illness, a shaman may be summoned at any time of the day or night. In this event, the doctoring begins as soon as the shaman arrives. Apparently these emergency treatments take place infrequently. The performance at night which is thought of by the Paviotso as the orthodox form of doctoring is called tuníku'hu (literally, singing). An emergency treatment which lasts about three hours is known as sɔgɔ́nǝbu'ᵘ. The meaning of this term is not known.

It is customary for the shaman to doctor a patient for two nights. Several informants insisted that the treatment must be kept up for this length of time even though the patient shows signs of recovery after the first night. The shaman does not doctor two successive nights, however, but rests one night between the first and second treatments. When a patient is dangerously ill, two shamans may be called in, though usually they do not work together, but alternately. One performs the first night and the other the second, and so on.

A member of the patient's family summons the shaman, usually visiting the shaman at sunrise. The shaman is reserved and aloof during the consultation, slowly smoking his pipe while considering the summoner's invitation. The fee is briefly discussed and agreed upon; it may also be paid at this time. In former days, beads, skins, blankets, and horses were paid for a shaman's services; nowadays the usual fee is three to five dollars. No doubt the shaman's remuneration varies considerably, the better-known practitioners charging even more than the larger sum mentioned.

It is said that shamans who overcharge their patients become ill. The explanation offered is that the shamans' powers determine the fee and if the practitioner asks for more the spirit will be angry and punish the offender. On the other hand, shamans are required by their powers to collect a fee for treating patients; the giving of free services would endanger the life of the shaman.

The only exception to this rule mentioned by informants is in the case of illness in the shaman's immediate family, where he can treat the sick without exacting a fee and at the same time remain in the good graces of his power.

Shamans may permit their patients to defer payment of the charges for curing. If the debt is not paid in a specified time, however, the shaman will suffer a serious illness. This is believed to be the shaman's penalty for disobeying the injunctions of his power. Consequently, the shaman makes sure that he will be paid, usually demanding the fee in advance. In spite of these precautions, several instances of sickness among shamans, attributed to the failure to pay, were recorded.

Shamans rarely refuse to accept a case. It is generally agreed that shamans are required to treat the sick whenever they are asked. It is said that if a shaman refuses to go, his power will be angry, and sickness and loss of power will result.

When invited to doctor, the shaman asks few questions. He does not inquire about the patient's symptoms, for his power is supposed to help him determine them. Yet he may briefly question the summoner about the patient's actions prior to the illness.

After gravely and quietly considering the request for assistance, the shaman announces that he will doctor that night. Then he directs the preparation of the stick (subínamadáʙu·inya) which is to be placed upright by the patient's head. The relative who summons the shaman cuts and prepares this stick, which is of willow and is three or four feet long. The shaman takes a feather from his kit (usually the tail-feather of the eagle) which, together with a bone or shell bead and down from the breast of the eagle, is attached by a buckskin thong to the blunt end of the stick. Red and white bands may also be painted on the wand. The precise way in which it is prepared and decorated depends upon the instructions received by the shaman in his dreams. The relative now returns home, and the wand that he has prepared under the direction of the shaman is stuck in the ground beside the patient's head with the feathers and the bead hanging by several inches of string from the top of the stick. During the day the wand may be kept outside the house, but it is taken in and placed by the patient before the doctoring begins.

The shaman arrives after dark, usually about nine o'clock. He is accompanied by his interpreter or "talker," called poínab°.[14] The interpreter, like the shaman, receives a fee for his services; usually he is paid about half as much as the shaman. His function in the curing rites is to repeat, in a loud clear voice, everything that is said by the shaman. In the curing rites, the shaman mumbles and speaks rapidly in broken snatches. The interpreter sitting at his left listens attentively and repeats the words clearly in order that the spectators may understand. He also follows the songs that the shaman sings, repeating the words loudly to enable the spectators to follow them easily and join in the singing. The interpreter learns only through practice, as he does not have supernatural power to aid him. A shaman always uses the same interpreter, who becomes familiar with his songs and way of talking. Several people stated that formerly the interpreters were not numerous, that shamans outnumbered interpreters. It is also said that in earlier days only men acted in this capacity, but nowadays women also interpret for shamans. One informant asserted that the interpreter also "prays" to the source of the sickness during the course of the curing. According to this statement, before the shaman starts to doctor, the interpreter seats himself by the patient and addresses the "sickness" with some such words as these:

> Our doctor is here. He is a good doctor. He is a strong doctor. You are poisoning this man. This doctor will find out about you. He knows you. Go away and leave this man alone. We do not want him to be sick. Go away and do not come back again. (Joe Green)

This informant stated that later in the performance, when the shaman had diagnosed the cause of illness, the interpreter again prays. This time he addresses the shaman. He might say,

> Cure this man. Make the sickness disappear. Make this man well. Suck out the sickness that is inside him. Show us the sickness that you suck out. Then he will recover.

Other informants did not confirm this function of the interpreter. The general opinion seems to be that the interpreter's duties consist only of repeating the words of the shaman and leading the spectators in singing his songs. Qualifications for this posi-

[14] It may be noted that a chief and the head man of a communal undertaking are also designated by the same term.

tion are a strong clear voice and the strength to continue singing throughout the entire night.

Still another assistant in the shamanistic performance is to be noted. This is the dancer (wütádᵘ). The dancer is always a woman and is said to be of necessity both good-looking and virtuous. She may be either married or single. This performer carries a bowl-shaped basket containing a number of pebbles or beads. This type of rattle (wədákətⁱ) is held close to the front of the body and jerked up and down in time to the dance step. The dancer follows the shaman at a distance of four or five feet when he gets up and dances around the fire in a counter-clockwise direction. Several said that the woman dances only with the shaman, but others stated that he may direct her to continue dancing while he is sucking the patient. The dance step is described as a short, quick jump. The dancer is paid for her services, receiving a fee equivalent to that of the interpreter.

Not all shamans employ dancers to assist in curing. It is difficult at the present time to determine the importance of these performers in the shamanistic performances of former times, but several informants agreed that under aboriginal conditions only a few shamans had women dance for them in the curing rite. The practice seems to have fallen into disuse, for several elderly people said that they had never seen a dancer perform at a doctoring; they had only heard of the custom. Apparently the dancer is always a woman; men never act in this capacity.

The shaman may not begin to doctor as soon as he arrives, for if it is still light he waits until darkness has settled. This means that in the summer the curing does not get under way before ten o'clock, as it is believed to be wrong to treat the sick in the twilight. On the other hand, a bright moon does not interfere with the curing performance. While waiting, the shaman may exchange gossip with spectators, but usually he sits quietly concentrating his thoughts on his power and the cause of the sickness.

When the shaman is ready to start the curing rites, he seats himself by the side of the patient. Moccasins or shoes have been previously removed. I failed to note whether the spectators are also barefoot. There is no general costume worn by shamans. One may be told in his dreams to wear feathers or to decorate his clothing in a particular way. Each shaman, therefore, has his own style of dots and lines of red and white paint applied to the face and body. The interpreter is seated usually at the shaman's left; the patient lies with his head to the south. Spectators range themselves along the walls of the house, grouped in several rows if they are numerous. Children are permitted to be present, but are required to be quiet. Only menstruating and pregnant women are excluded. The presence of the former is believed to be particularly dangerous, and no woman shaman in that condition would undertake a cure. It is said that a shaman can quickly detect the presence of a menstruating woman, for as soon as he starts to sing he becomes hoarse and shortly he is unable to talk or sing. He then demands that the guilty woman come forward, and she is required to decorate herself with red paint and to sprinkle some of it around the fire.

As soon as the shaman is seated by the patient, he takes his pipe, rattle, and other paraphernalia from his kit and lays them on the ground before him. Then he begins to sing softly without shaking the rattle. First comes a set of five songs, apparently to call the shaman's spirit helper. The shaman may smoke for a few minutes before he begins to sing, or he may wait until all the spectators are singing before he lights his pipe. When the spectators take up the singing at the beginning of the sixth song, the shaman picks up his rattle and shakes it in time with the singing. As soon as the interpreter hears the first song, he begins to sing loudly, and the spectators join in as rapidly as they learn the song. It is said that spectators know early in the evening whether the shaman is to succeed in curing the patient. If his performance is marked by gusto and enthusiasm, his power is thought to be sufficiently strong to overcome the cause of the illness.

The number of songs and their length vary with different shamans. Some claim that the songs come to them from their powers while they are doctoring and they cannot remember them afterwards. Dick Mahwee said that his songs came to him through the eagle-feather on the stick that is planted by the patient's head. Other shamans assert otherwise, testifying that their songs are derived directly from the powers and that the feather wand does not have any connection with the singing.

After singing for a time, the shaman gets up and walks or hops slowly around the fire in the center of the room. If he employs a dancer, she follows him around the room each time he makes a circuit. He always moves around the room counter-clockwise. In describing this part of the performances, one informant volunteered the remark, "The whirlwind always moves in that direction too." Unfortunately, I neglected to question others on this point.

When the shaman sits down, he takes up his pipe, already filled by the interpreter, takes several puffs, and then passes it around among the spectators, always in a counter-clockwise direction. Everyone must take one or two whiffs of smoke, the number varying according to the shaman's instructions. The singing continues while the shaman smokes and during the time the pipe is being passed around. If anyone refuses to smoke, the shaman stops the performance until that person can be made to conform to his request. Otherwise the curing will not be successful, and the shaman will suffer from the annoyance of his power. The pipe is usually circulated among the spectators at intervals ranging from half an hour to an hour as long as the curing rite continues, customarily until morning.

The nature of the disease determines to some extent the general plan of procedure. If the patient is unconscious and appears to be dead, it is obvious that he is suffering from soul loss. It is then imperative for the shaman to go into a trance (yáika)[15] as quickly as possible in order to find and return the soul before it has strayed too far. On the other hand, when disease results from other causes, the shaman may go into a trance in order to diagnose the illness and to confer with his power on the treatment. Whether or not the shaman goes into a trance for the latter purposes is said to be dependent upon the strength of his power.

The procedure for entering a trance varies considerably from one practitioner to another, but the following statement will serve to give an outline of generally accepted forms of practice. The shaman who goes into a trance first details five men to catch him as he staggers about the fire singing. They lower him to the ground

[15] Lowie, *Shoshonean Ethnography*, 294, gives the term *mugwamanaqᵢ* for this shamanistic trance. My informants were not familiar with this word.

and when he shows signs of returning to consciousness, they rub his limbs, especially the joints, with the feather wand. If the spirit of the shaman is returning with a lost soul, he can be heard talking with the soul as the spirits approach their respective bodies. When the shaman uses the trance for prognostic purposes, he will not only see the cause of illness but also signs which are interpreted as omens of recovery or of death. A trance of the latter kind was described by Dick Mahwee.

> I smoke before I go into the trance. While I am in the trance no one makes any noise. I go out to see what will happen to the patient. When I see a whirlwind I know that it caused the sickness. If I see the patient walking on grass and flowers it means that he will get well; he will soon be up and walking. When I see the patient among fresh flowers and he picks them it means that he will recover. If the flowers are withered or look as if the frost had killed them, I know that the patient will die. Sometimes in a trance I see the patient walking on the ground. If he leaves footprints I know that he will live, but if there are no tracks, I cannot cure him.
>
> When I am coming back from the trance I sing. I sing louder and louder until I am completely conscious. Then the men lift me to my feet and I go on with the doctoring.

Apparently today few shamans are able to induce a trance state in the curing performance. It is frequently said that in former times, however, shamans commonly went into trances in curative practice. It is now impossible to determine how important a rôle this played in the shamanistic rites of aboriginal days. It should be noted that usually no distinctions are made between those who go into trances and those who do not. Several informants were of the opinion that there was only a difference in degree —those who used the trance were the more powerful shamans.

As soon as the shaman returns to consciousness, he relates his experiences in the trance. The singing is then resumed. If the shaman has found that the sickness is due to the presence of a disease object, at this point in the ceremony he will attempt to extract it by suction. This part of the treatment is shown as nubu'u or as patɔzibúoịid. My notes fail to give any distinction between the two terms.

He sucks the part of the body which his diagnosis has shown to be the seat of the pain. Usually he applies his mouth to the patient's body, but some shamans use a bone or willow tube through which the disease is sucked. The blood and the cause of disease are sucked out through the unbroken skin, as the shaman never bites or cuts the patient's body. While the shaman is sucking, the interpreter and spectators continue to sing until he signals for them to stop by a vigorous shake of the rattle. The blood that is sucked from the patient is spat into a shallow hole scooped out in the earth floor beside the shaman. A new song is started by the shaman as soon as he spits out the blood. Then the pipe may be passed around again and he walks or dances around the fire several times before he applies himself to the sucking. This procedure is repeated a number of times before the disease-object is extracted.

When the shaman finally draws out the cause of sickness, he exhibits it to the spectators. He shows a pebble, a small black lizard, an insect, or a worm, which he claims caused the illness. The disease-object is then disposed of by putting it in the hole with the bad blood and covering all with dirt. Apparently it is no longer harmful. As far as could be determined, no particular time is specified in the curing rite for the shaman to succeed in sucking out the cause of illness. Singing and smoking are resumed as soon as the shaman disposes of the disease-object.

At about midnight there is an intermission in the curing performance lasting about a half-hour. At this time food provided by the patient's family is passed among the spectators. It is said that the particular kind of food is prescribed by the shaman when he agrees to doctor the patient. The basket containing the food is handed about in a counter-clockwise direction. Some shamans indicate the exact way in which the food may be eaten at this time. Care is taken in handling the food. None should be dropped on the ground or wasted; and the unconsumed left-overs are carefully buried. Usually the shaman does not partake of the midnight meal. He may, however, talk and even joke with the spectators while they are eating.

The shaman brings the ceremony to an end in the morning a little before daylight. Shamans often say that as day approaches their songs come to them very faintly; this is regarded as a signal given by the powers to stop. The shaman then gives the family instructions for the care of the patient. He may order the patient painted with simple designs or prescribe special foods. These prescriptions are revealed to the shaman by his power in the course of the curing rites.

When the doctoring is nearly over, some shamans tell the spectators to dance, following him counter-clockwise around the fire. The dancers on this occasion do not clasp hands as in the round dance. Apparently the dance step is simply a walk in time with the songs. The shaman continues to sing the same song for ten or fifteen minutes while the people follow him around the fire. According to one description, at the end of the dance all must shake their clothes, at the same time blowing on their arms. It is believed that an evil spirit causing the sickness is still in the house and these actions drive it away.

The feather wand is left beside the patient's head after the first night of curing. At the end of the second night the shaman removes his feathers and bead. The stick is them disposed of by a member of the patient's family. Usually it is placed under cool water, but it may be put in the heart of a clump of brush where it will be cool and safe from the filth of the coyote and dogs; it is essential that it be a cool place. If either the coyote or dog were to touch the discarded stick, the shaman would suffer sickness and loss of power.

The use of two native paints, red (pi·jəp^i) and white (i·bi), is very common in curing practices. Both of these paints are secured from natural deposits of earth. The uses to which the paints are put are manifold: the bodies and faces of both shamans and spectators are painted, the patient is sprinkled with the dry powder, and the feathers and the wand used in curing are painted. There are no fixed patterns that determine the way in which the paint is to be used, nor is one color preferred to the other. Either red or white paint, and often both, appears in every phase of the shaman's practice. The use of these paints, however, is by no means confined to curing rites. In daily life these paints are employed for utilitarian as well as ritual purposes, and bodily decoration with these paints is also common on social occasions. Nevertheless, the paints are thought to be very potent in aiding the recovery of the sick.

It should be mentioned that the sweat-bath is not associated with curing practices among the Paviotso. This is true both of shamanistic curative practices and the ordinary home remedies that are utilized. The Paviotso learned of the sweat-house and its use only recently, and it has never achieved an important place in the culture. Apparently sweating has more religious associations with the Surprise Valley band of the Northern Paiute.[16]

The shaman is not held responsible when the patient dies. His failure is believed to be due either to the stronger power of a sorcerer or to other factors over which he had no control. It is said that nowadays the fee is not returned when the cure is unsuccessful. Apparently the former practice was for the shaman to return the fee if the patient died within a day or two after the treatment. When death occurred at any later time no restitution was made.

Legerdemain is not generally characteristic of the shamanistic performance. Apparently the shamans of today perform no tricks when curing, but several informants recall that in the past some practised sleight-of-hand. One shaman walked around the fire holding a basket on his head. He announced when he sat down, that if pine-nuts were in the basket the patient would recover; if there were no pine-nuts, the patient would die. When he stopped moving about the fire he showed the people that pine-nuts had mysteriously appeared in the basket. Other tricks of a similar nature were performed by a few shamans. No swallowing acts are performed by the shamans.

Several informants reported that some shamans picked up hot coals during the performance. One was known to have taken a hot coal in his mouth. It turned to white paint which he spat into his hands and rubbed on the patient. At one point in the curing performance, another shaman held an iron knife in the fire. When the knife was hot he put it into his mouth and "it sizzled like a hot iron dipped in water." Still another exhibition with fire was given by a shaman to show that he had power to cure. Before he started to sing he thrust a bundle of reeds or brush into the fire. When the ends caught fire he licked them with his tongue. Walking on fire is unknown in Paviotso practice.

16 Kelly, *Surprise Valley Paiute*, 202–204.

These few tricks are about the extent of the shaman's legerdemain. It is evident that sleight-of-hand forms no important part of the shaman's stock-in-trade. Moreover, only a few shamans at any time employed such means to demonstrate their powers.

The small number of songs that were recorded have not been analyzed, but several general observations can be made. The words of a shaman's song often refer to the source of power. The songs are short; frequently they are not more than four or five words in length, with meaningless syllables often incorporated. The three shaman's songs published by Gilbert Natches illustrate these points. The songs are short, and mention curing or other attributes of the shaman's power. The words of one song, "the soul pursuing, the person's soul bring back," obviously refer to restoring a soul that has been lost.[17] The words of a single song are repeated as long as the shaman cares to continue, usually ten or fifteen minutes, sometimes even longer.

Shamans claim that they are not familiar with their songs before actually engaging in the performance of the curing rite. As we have seen, songs come to the practitioners from their powers when they are needed and cannot be recalled the next day. In the course of recording songs, three otherwise quite willing informants insisted that they were unable to recall their own songs, although they could remember those of other shamans. Evidently, shamans' songs differ from those sung at the round dance and for the hand-game, although there appears to be little difference in words. A number of informants unhesitatingly identified curing songs when reproduced on the phonograph, but authorship was not always recognized, and property rights in them never.

The following two accounts of shamanistic curing will illustrate several points in the procedure outlined above.

> Jackson Overton's father, Natches Overton, doctored my mother one time. I was sitting with my uncle. Natches smoothed the ground in front of us. Then he drew three circles in a row in the dirt. He said that he wanted a man to take off his shoes and stand with a foot in each of the end circles. My uncle took off his shoes and stood where Natches told him. After a while Natches told him to sit down. Then Natches sang. When he finished his song he told my uncle to scrape

[17] Natches, *Northern Paiute Verbs*, 259.

away the dirt in the circles. In the dirt of the first two circles he found nothing. In the third he found a small hard object that looked like a piece of copper. It was about the size of a ten-cent piece and there was a hole in the center. Natches then said, "I think this woman will recover." He told them to tie the small object to the top of my mother's head with her hair. He said that she must keep it there for ten days. The next morning she felt better. In seven or eight days she was almost well. On the tenth day she got up and walked. (Joe Green)

Captain Dave was almost dead. His mind was gone. Two shamans were doctoring him. They quit because they could do nothing for him. People brought Bull Tom to doctor Captain Dave. Bull Tom said, "I am going to lie down here. I am going to find him. His mind is already gone. Maybe I cannot find him. I do not know how long he has been gone. Maybe it is too long." Bull Tom was in a trance for a long time. Then he was heard talking softly. He was still a long way off. We heard him say, "Do not be afraid. We are going home. We are going back to your home. We will go from here over to that mountain. Your boy, your daughter, your wife are all there. We are going back and see all of them there. Do not look back. Bad animals are back there. Do not go back; we will be home soon." Then Bull Tom came out of his trance. He told Captain Dave's family to blow on the top of Captain Dave's head. Captain Dave woke up. He recognized all the people around him. Bull Tom turned the doctoring over to the other shamans then. Captain Dave recovered and lived for many years. (Joe Green)

Shamans cure wounds and injuries as well as illness. The treatment is substantially the same for all. Usually shamans suck out arrowheads and bullets. In case of internal injury they draw off the blood which is believed to prevent recovery. Certain shamans, such as Wovoka, are credited with unusually strong powers for curing the injured and the wounded. No particular source of power is associated with this form of practice; such shamans also cure disease.

War parties are often accompanied by at least one shaman. He takes part in the fighting, and only when hostilities are over does he treat the wounded. The shaman utilizes his power while on the war-path solely for purposes of doctoring. The only exception is the shaman whose power not only enables him to cure but also makes him invulnerable. Invulnerability is occasionally exhibited in peace-times simply to demonstrate the shaman's mastery of supernatural spirits. It is not probable that these public exhibitions were ever very common.

Fighting and treating the wounded are the shaman's only functions on the war-path. He does not invoke the aid of his powers for the success of the party, nor does he prophesy the outcome of the venture.

WEATHER-CONTROL AND CLAIRVOYANCE

Although the shaman's function is chiefly to cure disease, control of the elements, the ability to foretell future events, and the discovery of lost articles, are all within the ability of at least some shamans. Usually shamanistic manipulation of the weather serves no practical need.[18] Often it is simply a means of demonstrating the control of supernatural power. By waving a feather or by singing, shamans may cause the clear sky to become cloudy, the wind to blow, or rain to fall. They can also stop wind and rain or banish the clouds that they have brought. Although the predominant motive in weather-control is this exhibition of power, shamans have been known in the past to manipulate weather for the benefit of the community. This weather-control is chiefly concerned with causing changes in the elements in order to bring about a badly-needed run of fish in the rivers. It is said that fish may be induced to go up the river in the spring by causing the ice to melt or by bringing about a wind that will force them to the mouth of the river. When ice covers the rivers late in the spring, delaying the run of fish from the lakes, a shaman known to have control over the elements is asked to cause warm weather and rain to melt the ice. Only a few shamans, however, have this power.

> During the winter the river was frozen over. The men could not fish. In the spring the people were hungry. There were no fish in the river. There was too much ice. It was cold. The people talked about it. They were talking about asking a certain shaman here (Pyramid Lake) who could help them. He had the power to bring a warm wind that would melt the ice. They sent two or three men to the shaman. They asked him to make the wind blow. The shaman sang and the ice was made to melt. Then the fish started up the river. The people caught many of them. They paid the shaman with fish. Everyone gave him fish. If the

[18] A form of weather-control is practised at the social round dances. While the dancers are moving in a circle a headman, not necessarily one with supernatural power, walks around praying for rain in order to insure abundant wild products.

shaman asked for beads, skins, or flint when he brought the wind, he would spoil his power. He would lose his power if he did not obey his spirit. (Joe Green)

Some shamans, but not all, are able to foretell the future. Apparently even among those who are supposed to have the ability to predict future events the power is not frequently exercised. One shaman is reported to have foreseen the coming of the whites, and others have foreseen several serious epidemics.

Sarah Winnemucca mentions the shamans' gift of prophecy. She describes a dream of her father's in which the killing of the Indians by the whites was predicted.[19] Although Sarah does not specifically make a statement about her father's power, there is evidence both in her account and from my field notes that he was a shaman. On still another occasion, future events were revealed to Sarah's brother in a dream. When he awoke from the dream, the people were called together and the prophecy was related.[20]

All informants denied that shamans exercise their clairvoyant powers either on the warpath or on the eve of the departure of the war-party. In fact, aside from their rôles in treating the wounded and fighting shoulder to shoulder with other men, shamans have no outstanding position in battle or the preparations that precede it. On these occasions, the shaman's position is definitely subordinate to that of the war-leader or chief. This official may, however, owe his position to the possession of supernatural power which makes him invulnerable, hence a daring and fearless fighter, the qualifications for the leader of a war party. In Sarah Winnemucca's account there is a suggestion, not borne out by the above, that shamans previsioned the outcome of battles. At least her father on one occasion and her brother on another foretold from dream experiences the outcome of impending conflicts with the whites.[21]

In all these clairvoyant revelations, only harmful events such as sickness, warfare, and death are predicted. There is no indication that successful undertakings or happy events are previsioned. This characteristic of Paviotso clairvoyance may be related to

[19] Hopkins, *Life Among the Piutes*, 14–15.
[20] Ibid., 80.
[21] Ibid., 14, 80.

the danger and evil inherent in so much of the dream experiences.

The clairvoyant detection of theft and the finding of lost or stolen property is within the scope of a few shamans, but as with other non-curing aspects of shamanistic functions, this is not widely practised. Several informants gave anecdotal accounts of these practices, but others seemed to think that such powers were not within the scope of shamanistic activities. Certainly invoking clairvoyant powers to track down a thief or to locate misplaced belongings played only a minor rôle in Paviotso life.

There is no evidence that clairvoyants have power that differs from the supernatural gifts of other shamans. It is more in the nature of a frill added by some shamans to the chief calling, that of curing.

Antelope Shamans

Communal activities play an important rôle in the economic life of the Paviotso. A large share of the meat supply is secured by drives in which a number of individuals participate. There is a stereotyped form of drive for rabbits, for mud hens, and for antelope. A leader or head-man, elected or chosen for each drive, is responsible for the direction of the undertaking.

These communal drives, like every other phase of Paviotso life, are tinged with religious belief and practice. The religious rites that must accompany daily activities are usually extremely simple, consisting of prayers and the observation of omens. The shaman does not take a leading part in these unelaborated practices. With the antelope-drive, however, the case is different, for a shaman directs the activities of all who take part. Moreover, the success of the undertaking is dependent upon a shamanistic performance, which precedes the actual drive.

The shaman who is leader of the drive must have the spirit of the antelope as his source of power. This power is secured in one of the customary ways described previously. Apparently only men are antelope shamans, but in Paviotso theory, women may enjoy this as well as other powers. Shamans with power from the antelope frequently cure, in addition to charming antelope in the communal drive. Other spirits may be invoked in curing practice, but only the antelope spirit is of assistance in charming the animals. An antelope shaman who also treats the sick is known as puhágəm or tunápuhágəm (tuná, antelope; puhágəm, shaman). If the antelope-charmer does not have curative powers, this term is not used; in fact there seems to be no word to designate the non-curing antelope shaman.

Almost no one living today has participated in an antelope-drive, as these have not been held for many years. The information that the older people could offer was derived largely from memories of the conversations and stories of a generation now dead. As might be expected, there are striking differences in the several accounts, but the generalized description given here includes the essential features without the variations in detail included in the versions given by several informants.

The antelope-drive is called by a shaman who has the antelope spirit as power. He first sends out scouts to find a herd of antelope, but if anyone sees a herd he may go to an antelope shaman and tell him where the animals are. Some shamans are said to find the antelope herds simply by dreaming. In the spring, when food supplies are exhausted, there is often a strong public demand for the antelope shaman to exercise his power.

When the herd of antelope has been found, the procedure is first to build a corral of sagebrush-bark rope under the direction of the antelope shaman at a place which he has previously selected. A corral may be used a number of times, but it is the property of the shaman who directed the construction; at least other shamans make no use of it. When the rope has been prepared beforehand, the corral can be finished in a day. That night a dance is held either at the camp established near by or within the corral. Apparently there is no fixed rule for the length of the dance: several said that it lasts only a few hours, others that it is not over until morning. In the latter event, the dancers go out at daylight to drive in the antelope. During the dance the shaman sings his antelope-songs, goes into a trance, or otherwise performs in order to charm the antelope and make them docile when they are driven into the corral.

Music for the singing and dancing in the charming rite is frequently provided by rubbing a rasp made by wrapping a bow-string around a piece of horn. The notched-stick rasp was reported by two informants. Several others told of rubbing an arrow across a taut bowstring to provide musical accompaniment for the singing and dancing. The rattles customarily employed in the curing ceremony seem never to be used in charming antelope.

Early in the morning, when the dance is finished, the drive starts. Some people are stationed along the flaring wings of the corral, while others drive the herd between the converging lines into the corral. When the herd is safely inside, the entrance is closed. The participants are stationed around the corral in order to keep the antelope from breaking down the fence. Usually the killing does not take place until the following day. In the meantime, the guards build fires around the corral and keep a careful watch.

On the morning of the next day, a man noted as a runner enters the corral and drives the antelope around within the enclosure for several hours. The runner finally kills a young antelope, which he gives to the antelope shaman. Then the signal is given by the leader of the drive for the killing to begin; the animals are dispatched by hand. Each individual is regarded as the owner of all that he kills. A woman or an older child who does not have the strength to kill an antelope touches one or holds to some part of it until a man can offer assistance. By thus touching or holding an animal, ownership is established.

The first antelope killed as well as those dispatched by his own hands belong to the antelope shaman. He expects no pay nor any share in the animals killed by others as a reward for his services. The heads of all the antelope killed are collected and roasted in communal pits and shared by all; they are not given to the shaman as his fee.

When the skull has been cleaned of all flesh, the bones, together with the jaw-bone, are hidden in a clump of sagebrush. This is believed to assure the success of future drives. Some informants said that the eyes are tied in pairs and hung on trees or buried in the ground where dogs and coyote cannot get at them. The bladder, si·nupⁱ, and a small pear-shaped organ, abui'wi (spleen?), are put into a hole and covered with dirt. The careful disposal of certain parts of the animal is not confined to the antelope-drive. When other large game, such as deer and mountain sheep, are killed, the hunter treats these organs and bones in the same way in order to protect his luck for future hunting. Moreover, every part of the carcass must be used, for if any of the flesh is wasted, the antelope will be angry and may not allow themselves to be seen and killed.

Men, women, and childran participate in the antelope-drive. Only women who are pregnant or menstruating are excluded. It is believed that the presence of a woman in either of these conditions causes the antelope to break through the corral fence and escape. Several informants said that the husbands of menstruating and pregnant women were also prohibited from taking part in the drive.

When the antelope shaman calls people together for a drive, he warns them about their behavior. Sexual intercourse among the married is forbidden during the several days required to build the corral. The tabu on sexual relations lasts until the antelope have been slaughtered. It is also forbidden for young people to flirt. People participating in the drive are not supposed to relieve themselves anywhere near the fence of the corral. The loss of any personal property within the corral is believed to weaken the fence; consequently everyone is warned to watch personal possessions carefully. These rules and prohibitions are not in force during the communal hunts held for other game.

Both Sarah Winnemucca and Lowie give details of the antelope drive. In general, the plan of procedure outlined by these writers is similar to that given here. According to Sarah Winnemucca, the antelope-charming lasted for five days, during which people were not to drop anything or stumble over sagebrush, and were to concentrate their thoughts on the antelope.[22] Features in her account unknown to informants today include a definite plan of the camp in which the participants stay, the corral composed only of mounds of stone and sagebrush a hundred yards apart with no fence between, the selection of two men as messengers to the antelope carrying large torches of sagebrush, and the encircling of the herd by the messengers on each of the five days that the performance lasted.[23] The "kind of drum" which is described is

[22] Hopkins, *Life Among the Piutes*, 56.
[23] Ibid., 55–57.

but an elaborately constructed rasp.[24] The skin stuffed with grass around which cord is wound serves as a resonator when the rasp is rubbed with a stick.

One of Lowie's informants describes a drive lasting three days. The shaman and two assistants wear antelope-heads and paint themselves for a dance. A notched stick is rasped for music. During the ceremony, a shaman goes into a trance and imitates the call of the antelope. When the antelope are surrounded, two or three antelope are killed first and given to the shaman and his assistants.[25]

It is clear that the antelope shaman's performance has an important place in the shamanistic complex of the Paviotso. But as has been pointed out, the charming of game through the exercise of the shaman's power is confined entirely to the antelope-drive. The plan of procedure is highly variable, but the basic belief in the control of the antelope by supernatural power is clear. Antelope-charming, then, is the one well-recognized function of the shaman which is not a part of the all-pervading belief in curing. In fact, it is the only important shamanistic performance of the Paviotso that is not heavily charged with beliefs about the cause and control of disease.

The Position of the Shaman in the Social Order

At this late date, an assessment of the position of the shaman in Paviotso society is difficult. The social disintegration that has resulted from reservation life has destroyed much of the shaman's social influence and prestige. Consequently his part in the social fabric and in the daily life of aboriginal times can at best only be inferred.

There can be no doubt that the shaman was formerly an influential figure; the stronger his supernatural power the greater his social prestige. Thus the influence that he exerted was by no means confined to religious affairs and activities. A comparison of his social and political authority with that of the chief is, however, difficult, for any weighting of the respective importance of these officials is strange to Paviotso thinking. Certainly, in many in-

---

[24] Ibid., 56.
[25] Lowie, *Shoshonean Ethnography*, 304–305.

stances, the two offices are closely linked, as is indicated in the past by the appreciable number of prominent chiefs who also possessed and exercised shamanistic power. Such outstanding chiefs in historical times as both of the famous Winnemuccas, Captain Dave, and others, were known alike for their curative powers and for their ability to influence and lead their tribesmen. There is a suggestion in this and other evidence that a large proportion of the chiefs in pre-Caucasian times had supernatural powers which they used in curing practices. Nevertheless, supernatural experience is not necessary for chieftainship. Influential secular leaders without shamanistic qualifications are recalled, but according to one account "the power helped."

Not every powerful shaman, on the other hand, became a chief. Although holding no official political office, shamans were frequently consulted on secular affairs, and their opinions were respected. One case will illustrate the influential position of shamans. Wovoka, the leader of the 1890 Ghost Dance movement, was well known in his later years as a shaman with unusually strong power for curing disease. At the same time, his counsel was often sought in other matters. Clearly, he wielded greater influence over the Paviotso than did any of the contemporary chiefs; but in spite of this unofficial recognition and the great prestige that he enjoyed among his people, Wovoka was not looked upon as a chief nor did he ever claim the title.

There can be no doubt that the coming of the whites was responsible for substantially increasing the importance and influence of the chief. This official represented his people in dealings with the aliens, and later under reservation conditions he was given a small stipend and his authority was thereby appreciably enhanced. In aboriginal times, it was unquestionably the shaman who played the more important rôle in the social life. Of course the combined shaman-headman enjoyed perhaps even greater respect and influence than a political figure without supernatural power or a practitioner without chiefly title or office.

The position of the shaman, like that of any other member of Paviotso society, depends entirely upon individual abilities and accomplishments. Although shamanistic power may be inherited, the position and prestige of a powerful shaman are not transmitted to his heirs. One who inherits power of an outstanding and influential shaman may be only an obscure and indifferent practitioner. It must also be remembered that shamans have no organization or society through which the shaman's religious and social authority may be strengthened and consolidated. The shaman acquires his power, performs his rites, and attains his position only by individual initiative and achievement. Evidence points to a strong rivalry among shamans rather than to common interests and coöperative effort. This leads apparently to jealousies and efforts to overcome rivals by witchcraft.

In daily life the shaman follows the same pursuits as those who are less gifted with supernatural power. The men hunt, fish, and carry on the other usual masculine activities. The women gather seeds, prepare food, and perform similar customary tasks allotted to Paviotso women. The shaman does not use any of the wealth acquired from his shamanistic fees to satisfy his daily needs. The idea of buying and selling food, for example, is totally strange to the Paviotso. Hence a shaman must provide his food, clothing, and shelter by the same efforts that are of major concern in the daily routine of the less supernaturally favored.

The shaman is not excluded from the lighter recreations of his fellow men. To be sure he is somewhat reserved: he does not joke, laugh loudly, or act boisterously. He is usually quiet and serious when in the presence of others. Nevertheless, he joins in the perpetual gambling games, and he is free to take part in the social dances if he so desires.

More than anyone else, shamans have the opportunity to gain wealth. The beads, skins, and horses that are highly prized are acquired from patients. Accumulated wealth is of little value, however. Skins are used for clothing, and consequently shamans are in a position to display somewhat better garments than others, but to the Paviotso way of thinking, the accumulation of extensive resources is not desirable. Food, as has been mentioned, is not a commodity and hence cannot be purchased. Moreover, a large amount of property might at times even be a handicap in the frequent shifting of camp so typical of Paviotso habits. The property that the shaman acquires from his practice can, then, be used chiefly for gambling stakes. Largely because of this popu-

lar form of recreation, economically valuable objects are kept in
constant circulation. The shaman, therefore, sets no great store
by a large amount of property, nor can he be characterized as an
individual of wealth.

There is no evidence that the shaman's house differs in any
detail from the usual habitations. The size of the house depends
more on the number of occupants and their care and skill in
building, than on social position. The shaman does not decorate
his house or otherwise distinguish it with marks or signs of his
profession. Feathers, stuffed birds, animals, or other symbols of
his power are not put up either outside or inside the dwelling.

There is some reason to believe that the person of the shaman
is considered, often in a vague way, somewhat sacred and consequently dangerous. The fear of harming a shaman by awakening
him before his wandering soul can return has already been mentioned. In addition to being regarded with awe tinged with fear,
the shaman is also treated with respect, which again in part may
be due to fear. If a shaman is annoyed by disrespectful behavior,
he may practise sorcery against the offender; consequently care is
taken never to offend him. On the other hand, the fear and respect
felt for the shamans probably are related in part to the general
feeling that there is latent danger in anything connected with
supernatural forces.

There is an unformulated belief in the supernatural potency of
both the shaman's person and his soul. This attitude is reflected
in the testimony of several informants that when shamans die,
clouds gather in the sky, rain falls, or other changes in the weather
take place. Another asserted that earthquakes mark a shaman's
death. There were other witnesses who denied the existence of
such beliefs. According to Paviotso belief, births and deaths
among laymen are never accompanied by any changes in the
weather.

As the origins of both the 1870 and 1890 Ghost Dance movements are traced to the Paviotso, it may be of interest to estimate
the position in the society of the various leaders of these movements. Four prophets who announced the imminent return of the
dead and held dances to facilitate that event are distinctly remembered today; possibly there were others. At the time that they

preached their doctrines, the prophets were not shamans, i.e., they did not have power to cure. But all, of course, had had visionary experiences and, therefore, were apart from normal individuals. Apparently when a messiah declined in favor, because of his inability to bring about the promised resurrection, he acquired power to cure disease. Several of these prophets became powerful doctors in their later years and were much in demand for their curative abilities.

The social position of the prophet is rather difficult to reconstruct on the basis of present conditions alone. Evidence suggests, however, that Ghost Dance leaders did not become chiefs; in fact the vested interests of the chiefs and the well-established shamans were the source of the strongest opposition. In spite of this resistance, the prophets appear to have exerted considerable influence and caused a great flurry of excitement for short periods; then followed a marked decline in public interest when they failed to produce results. At least two prophets later regained much of their earlier prestige through the demonstration of great power in curing. One of these, Wovoka, was a powerful and influential figure among the Paviotso. He was held in high esteem by members of all the bands, and five years after his death, he was spoken of by nearly all Paviotso with admiration and respect. Perhaps some of the influence he enjoyed in later years among his own people can be traced to the demand by other Indians for his advice on religious matters.

Apparently the more important Ghost Dance prophets were at first rebels who made their revolts felt for only a short time. Later when his movement collapsed, the prophet found an acceptable substitute in exploiting the traditional pattern of shamanism. Probably these individuals added something to the old content and interpretation of shamanistic practice and belief. At all events, prophets were clearly respected and their pronouncements considered carefully, for they were people charged with supernatural power, and hence not to be safely ignored or offended.

It is evident, then, that the Paviotso shaman enjoys an important and respected position in society. It cannot be said that his influence is greater than the chief's, for often one man is both chief and shaman. Moreover, the shaman has an opportunity to acquire wealth, but the social values do not foster the development of a wealthy class. His power, wealth, and position, therefore, do not relieve him of the everyday pursuits in gaining a livelihood. In short, his supernatural power does not offer the opportunity to gain marked economic privileges.

Summary

The Paviotso shamanistic complex is seen to consist of an array of simple beliefs and practices. The dominant idea in shamanism is that of curing diseases; all other aspects are secondary.

Although the chief ceremonial performance of the Paviotso is the curing rite, this is a simple affair with a minimum of public participation. Singing, dancing, and smoking, with occasional crude sleight-of-hand tricks, are combined in a rite definitely lacking in complexity. This constitutes almost the entire ceremonial life of the Paviotso.

In spite of this meager content and marked simplicity of organization, Paviotso practice and belief are striking in several features. The emphasis on involuntary experiences both in acquiring power and in causing disease, the frequent lack of overt acts in the practice of sorcery, and the orientation of nearly all shamanistic ceremony around the control of disease, clearly indicate the focal point of interest in the Paviotso complex.

The important antelope-charming performance is the only exception to this concern of shamanistic activity with control of disease. But even here many beliefs involve those clustering about curing. The antelope shaman acquires power and exercises it in almost the same fashion as the practitioner; often, in fact, both functions are performed by one person.

In many of its aspects Paviotso shamanism may then be regarded as having a basis of generalized simple elements; but in emphasis on particular ideas of disease and curing, in peculiarity of interpretation of certain other traits, and in some novel combinations of practices found widely over western North America, the Paviotso complex presents at least several features that are unique.

III. The Shamanistic Complex in Western North America

It is my purpose in the present chapter to show the distribution in the Great Basin, California, and in the Plateau of those elements of Paviotso shamanism shared with the tribes of these areas. Although shamanistic practices and beliefs may present a fairly uniform picture over most of western North America, many of the elements in the Paviotso complex have different distributions in this region. With these distributions before us, it will be possible to indicate some of the cultural interrelations that have contributed to the growth of Paviotso shamanism. Moreover, we shall be in a position to show how the elements distributed among neighboring tribes have entered into combinations among the Paviotso that are different from the associations of traits found elsewhere. Finally, some of the elements in the Paviotso complex that are the result of local growth may be indicated.

An examination of the distributional evidence is limited, of course, by the material available. Limitations are especially evident in the information on shamanism for the tribes of western North America. In no other phase of culture does there seem to be such a paucity of adequate and uniform data even for those groups for which we have ethnographic descriptions.[1] Spier has briefly evaluated the literature on the Plateau tribes,[2] and today the situation is substantially the same with additional material available only in Ray's satisfactorily full account of the Sanpoil and Nespelem and an excellent but as yet unpublished manuscript on the Southern Okanagon.[3]

The Great Basin tribes are almost entirely unknown. The only published data that we have are Lowie's avowedly incomplete notes and the valuable material recently published on Chemehuevi

[1] The ethnographic accounts upon which the present distributional analysis is based have been supplemented by important unpublished material. I wish to acknowledge my indebtedness to Dr. Edward Sapir, Dr. Leslie Spier, Dr. G. P. Murdock, Dr. E. A. Hoebel, Dr. W. W. Hill, Mrs. Nan Cooke, Mr. Jack Harris, and Mr. Marvin K. Opler for generously making their field data available.

[2] Spier, *Klamath Ethnography*, 224–225.

[3] By Cline and others (see bibliography). Made available to me through the kindness of the editor, Dr. Leslie Spier.

practices by Kelly. Lowie's notes are on two Southern Paiute bands—the Moapa and the Shivwits—the Paviotso, the Ute bands that he visited at Navaho Springs and Ignacio in Colorado and at Whiterocks in Utah, and the Wind River Shoshoni of Wyoming. The Lemhi Shoshoni[4] are only briefly described, but probably have a basic Great Basin culture with only a recent overlay of some Plains traits. Supplementary data have been derived from several unpublished sources, such as Sapir's field notes on the Kaibab, and Hoebel's unpublished manuscript on the shamanism of a band of Northern Shoshoni known as "Seed Eaters," whose aboriginal habitat was on Bannock Creek, a tributary of the Snake River, in the southern part of the present Fort Hall Reservation in Idaho.

The recent field work carried on by Harris will supply much needed information on two Basin groups, the Tosawi[hi] or White Knives, a band occupying a large territory to the east and northeast of the Paviotso country, and the Salmon Eaters, who lived along the Snake River in the neighborhood of Twin Falls and Glen's Ferry. In pre-reservation days, the territories of the two bands seem to have overlapped somewhat. Ethnographic data bear out the anticipated similarities in these cultures.[5]

The four bands of Southern Ute studied by Opler indicate a situation similar to that of the Lemhi Shoshoni, a Basin culture in many phases of life with a relatively recent overlay of Plains elements. The Ute groups investigated by Opler ranged in aboriginal times south of the Gunnison River and generally south of a line roughly drawn from Gunnison National Park eastward to Denver.[6]

Kelly's account of the Surprise Valley Paiute and Steward's report on the Owens Valley Paiute describe groups that, although located in California, belong both in habitat and cultures to the western margin of the Great Basin. The Surprise Valley band, through constant inter-communication, was especially closely re-

[4] The group described by Lowie in the *Northern Shoshone*. The recent and as yet unpublished material collected by Hoebel indicates a number of culturally distinct bands that have heretofore been subsumed under the headings Northern Shoshone, Lemhi Shoshone, and Wind River Shoshone.

[5] Harris, *Field notes*, ms.

[6] Opler, *Ute field notes*, ms.

lated to the Paviotso, as it was also apparently connected with the Oregon Paiute. Contact between the Paviotso and the Owens Valley Paiute people was likewise close.

This leaves several large blocks of tribes or bands in the Great Basin that are wholly or almost wholly unknown: the Western Shoshoni bands, the Oregon Paiute, the Bannock, a large number of bands in eastern Nevada and in Utah west of the Great Salt Lake, most of the numerous groups of both Northern and Southern Ute, and finally several of the Southern Paiute bands for which Kelley's material is not yet available. Although the Great Basin is at present largely a blank area on the cultural map of North America, the field studies of Steward, Harris, Opler, Cooke and others promise to fill in many of the important gaps in the ethnographic record. Anticipating fuller knowledge of these cultures, it may be possible to suggest some of the significant relationships of the Paviotso shamanistic complex to practices of neighboring peoples.

Even with the intensive investigations that have been carried on among the tribes of California, information on the shamanistic practices is scanty. Perhaps an interest in the cults and other striking phases of the California cultures has resulted in the neglect of the humbler aspects of shamanism. At any rate, no treatment of shamanism in California, with the exception of Du Bois' study of the Wintu, is as complete as several that are available for Plateau tribes such as the Sanpoil and Nespelem, or the Klamath.

Therefore when we consider the literature on most of the interior tribes of western North America, great as the gaps are in the Plateau region, information is more nearly complete for that area than for either the Great Basin or California. It must be remembered, however, that this appraisal of the literature on these two areas applies only to the data on shamanism. This must be added to the earlier statement that cultural investigations in the Great Basin lag far behind the work in either of the other two areas.

However scanty and unsatisfactory the literature on much of the Basin and neighboring areas may be, the importance of shamanistic belief and practice in the religious activities has often been noted. As we have seen, shamanism bulks large in the ceremonial life of the Paviotso, where other rites are meager or entirely lacking. This situation probably prevails throughout most of the Great Basin; it is certainly true of the closely related peoples of Owens and Surprise valleys. In the east, among the Ute and Northern Shoshoni groups, where the Sun Dance has been recently introduced, there is, to be sure, an overlay of these other ceremonies. Still shamanism continues to figure here as a very significant part of the religious life.

Turning to the interior tribes of Washington and Oregon, we again find the religion dominated by shamanistic beliefs and practices. Some of the influences on these cultures, emanating from the more complex civilizations of the Northwest Coast, have been suggested by Spier.[7] It is in the southern Plateau that reflections of these forces seem to be less apparent. This and other evidence of differences between the northern and southern cultures of this region favor Spier's statement, "It was, and is, my contention that the typical forms of Plateau culture are to be found in the southern part of that area rather than in the north."[8] And it is precisely among the tribes in the south that religion centers so largely in shamanism.

In northern California the rôle of the shaman in the religious and social structure is important, but with other religious rites also prominent. Still further south, in the north central part of the state, the shamanistic complex is overshadowed by the Kuksu cult rites. Nevertheless, in this more complex religion, as Kroeber and Loeb have indicated, there is certainly a suggestion of an historical relation to shamanism.[9] With the Yokuts, and the more southerly tribes of California, strong emphasis on shamanism again emerges, although in this area such rites as the initiation ceremonies also figure prominently in tribal interests.

Religion, then, over a substantial part of western North America, centers largely in shamanism; but, as has been suggested before, the shamanistic complex throughout this region is not identical either in content or interpretation, and the distributions of certain practices and beliefs that have been reported for the several tribes will throw light on both the unique features

[7] Spier, *Klamath Ethnography*, 241 f.
[8] Cline and others, *Southern Okanagon*, ms., Preface by Leslie Spier.
[9] Kroeber, *Handbook*, 373, 859; Loeb, *Pomo Folkways*, 355, 366, 402.

of local practice and the inter-relationships of elements occurring widely in western North America.

SOURCE OF POWER

As we have seen, the Paviotso shaman derives supernatural power from a host of spirits. The spirits of animals, birds, snakes, and even fish are the sources of shamans' powers. In a few cases, power is also secured from natural phenomena such as clouds, thunder, etc. In addition, the dwarf-like beings which inhabit the lakes and water-holes are sources of spiritual aid, as are the ghosts of the dead.

The belief in the spirits of animals and natural phenomena as the source of supernatural power is widespread over western North America. Details are lacking for most of the Great Basin, but the Owens Valley Paiute, Surprise Valley Paiute, Kaibab, Chemehuevi, Northern and Southern Ute, Wind River and Lemhi Shoshoni, the Salmon Eater and White Knives bands of Shoshoni, all specifically secure power from these sources.[10]

In the Plateau area and southward into California, the concept of power derived from animal spirits and natural phenomena is well developed. All the tribes for which we have available material in this region have the belief that power comes from a host of spirits. This is clearly the case with the Thompson, Lillooet, Shuswap, Southern Okanagon, Sanpoil and Nespelem, Tenino, Klallam, the Salish tribes of Puget Sound, Wishram, Nez Percé, Takelma, Klamath, Wintu, Achomawi, Atsugewi, Northern Maidu.[11]

There are local differentiations and specializations, however, in the particular spirit or class of spirits from which power is secured. Among the Thompson, for example, the sun, stars, and the Milky

[10] Steward, *Owens Valley Paiute*, 308 f.; Kelly, *Surprise Valley Paiute*, 190; *Chemehuevi Shamanism*, 129; Sapir, *Kaibab field notes*, ms.; Densmore, *Northern Ute Music*, 127; Opler, *Southern Ute field notes*, ms.; Lowie, *Northern Shoshone*, 224 f.; *Shoshonean Ethnography*, 296; Hoebel, *Shoshone Religion*, ms.; Harris, *Field notes*, ms.

[11] Teit, *The Thompson Indians*, 354–355; *The Lillooet*, 283; *The Shuswap*, 605–610; Cline and others, *Southern Okanagon*, ms.; Ray, *The Sanpoil and Nespelem*, 172 f.; Murdock, *Tenino field notes*, ms.; Gunther, *Klallam Ethnography*, 291 f.; Haeberlin, *SbEtEdáꝘ*, 250; Spier and Sapir, *Wishram Ethnography*, 236 f.; Spinden, *The Nez Percé*, 247 f.; Sapir, *Religious Ideas of the Takelma*, 35; Spier, *Klamath Ethnography*, 100 f.; Du Bois, *Wintu Ethnography*, 113 f.; Dixon, *Notes on the Achomawi and Atsugewi*, 218; Angulo, *Religious Feeling*, 356; Park, *Atsugewi field notes*, ms.; Dixon, *The Northern Maidu*, 281.

Way were, with natural phenomena and animals, the favorite guardian spirits of shamans; with the Sanpoil and Nespelem heavenly bodies were not a source of power and natural phenomena only occasionally so. Still another illustration of local interpretation is found in the beliefs of the latter two tribes. The notion is held among these people that an indefinitely large number of animal spirits and natural phenomena give supernatural power, and although these spirits were never human they always assumed human form when they appeared before people.[12] Again, parts of an animal or an object such as the nose or tail of a deer, the nipple of a gun, or the left or right side of anything may be the source of supernatural power. This conception is most clearly formulated among the Thompson, Lillooet, and Shuswap.[13]

The Paviotso do not acquire power solely from these spirits. It has been mentioned that water-babies are also a common source of supernatural aid. The conception of dwarf-like people acting as guardian spirits or giving power is widespread west of the Rocky Mountains. In the Great Basin, the concept is reported for the Northern Ute, where a shaman stated that, "he treated the sick under the tutelage of a 'little green man' and that numerous other medicine men were under the same guidance, there being many of the little green men." These dwarfs are described as about two feet in height, green from head to foot, and carrying a bow and arrows. The arrows are shot into anyone who speaks unkindly of them. The little green men live in the mountains. They are the guardians of the "medicine men," those who cure entirely by supernatural power, especially cases resulting from witchcraft, in contrast to the "doctors," who have power from birds and animals and cure by aid of supernatural power in addition to the use of herbal medicines which have been revealed to them.[14]

Dwarfs living in the mountains, and water-babies are known as a source of power among the Wind River Shoshoni, several of the Northern Shoshoni bands at Fort Hall, the White Knives, and the Salmon Eaters. One of these bands, the Seed Eaters, hold

[12] Teit, *The Thompson Indians*, 354; Ray, *The Sanpoil and Nespelem*, 172–173.
[13] Teit, *The Thompson Indians*, 355; *The Lillooet*, 283; *The Shuswap*, 609–610.
[14] Densmore, *Northern Ute Music*, 127 f.

that the strongest power is derived from ghosts and mountain-dwelling dwarfs, and, as with the neighboring groups, water-babies also confer power. Gifford has noted the occurrence of the belief that water-babies are "malevolent sprites" in the mythology of several Shoshonean groups, Western Mono, Paiute of central Oregon, Northern Shoshoni, and Serrano. He finds such notions absent in typical central Californian groups.[15]

Dwarfs are reported for several of the Plateau groups: Thompson, Shuswap, Southern Okanagon, Klamath, and the Tenino of Warm Springs. Only the Thompson among those in the northern part of the area believe that the dwarfs may act as guardian spirits. The Klamath and Tenino secure supernatural power from dwarfs; one is a water-dwelling dwarf, according to the conception of the Klamath.[16]

In northern California, the conception of dwarfs as a source of power is characteristic of the Shasta, Atsugewi, Northern Maidu, and Yuki, with the more elaborate development of the belief occurring among the Shasta. Here the Axeki or "pains" are conceived of as human in form, "rather shorter than the ordinary stature." They inhabit rocks, streams, lakes, and mountains, the sun, moon, and some stars. A large number of animals as well are thought to be Axeki. "They are the cause of all disease, death, and trouble, and become the guardians of the shamans, and are often inherited by them."[17]

Spier has suggested that these dwarf-like spirits are related in some way to the beings, such as the ghosts of the dead that appear in dreams among the Yurok and Sinkyone, from whom other northern Californians derive power.[18] I do not think that a connection is established in the face of the wide occurrence of dwarfs and water-babies in the Great Basin, among the Klamath, and when the unbroken distribution into northeastern California (Atsugewi, Northern Maidu, etc.) is considered. It seems evident that this source of power belongs largely to the Great Basin and

[15] Lowie, *Shoshonean Ethnography*, 296 f.; Hoebel, *Shoshone Religion*, ms.; Harris, *Field notes*, ms.; Gifford, *Western Mono Myths*, 304.

[16] Teit, *The Thompson Indians*, 339; *The Shuswap*, 599; Cline and others, *The Southern Okanagon*, ms.; Spier, *Klamath Ethnography*, 104 f.; Murdock, *Tenino field notes*, ms.

[17] Dixon, *Shasta*, 470, 476; Park, *Atsugewi field notes*, ms.; Dixon, *Northern Maidu*, 265; Kroeber, *Handbook*, 198.

[18] Spier, *Klamath Ethnography*, 246.

northern California, with the Klamath and Tenino sharing the notion. In addition, we find the beliefs of dwarfs and certain mythical beings known also to several Plains groups. The Crow, to cite one case, believe in a uniformly benevolent dwarf who appears in visions.[19] Despite the wide distribution of the belief in dwarfs, the conception of such beings as a source of power is definitely localized. In other words, the presence of the belief in dwarfs is not enough to justify regarding them as sources of power. It may be noted that a belief in water-monsters, generally conceived of as malevolent, is widespread in the Plateau and northern California, but I am unable to find any evidence that they were generally a source of power even among such a group as the Thompson, where the spirit sources of power embrace a vast array of animals, beings, and natural phenomena. Power is acquired from water-monsters, however, among the Yokuts, Wishram, and Tenino, who regard long-haired beings that live in the water as a source of supernatural aid.[20]

The concept of power derived from ghosts or spirits of dead relatives appears on the western edge of the Great Basin only among the Paviotso, so far as we know. In the east, among the Shoshoni Seed Eaters, ghosts are the source of the strongest power; with the Salmon Eater band these spirits confer only the ability to cure those affected by them.[21] Unfortunately, there is no information for the intervening area. The evidence for a connection between these widely separated appearances of the conception is, therefore, far from satisfactory.

Among the interior tribes of Oregon and Washington, with few exceptions ghosts are not regarded as a source of shamanistic power. The Klamath may possibly differ in this respect, for it is noted that curing is possible only through certain spirits, among them "a woman spirit."[22] On the other hand, among the Tenino, ghosts unquestionably confer special power for curing.[23] Still another exception is found in the north with the Lillooet and Thompson,

[19] Lowie, *Religion of the Crow Indians*, 322.

[20] Kroeber, *Handbook*, 504; Spier and Sapir, *Wishram Ethnography*, 236, 238; Murdock, *Tenino field notes*, ms.

[21] Hoebel, *Shoshone Religion*, ms.; Harris, *Field notes*, ms.

[22] Spier, *Klamath Ethnography*, 123.

[23] Murdock, *Tenino field notes*, ms.

among whom ghosts of the dead are guardian spirits of shamans.[24]

In northern California the concept of power derived from the spirits of the dead appears in full force. The Yurok shaman dreams of a dead person, usually, if not always, of one who has been a shaman. The Sinkyone sometimes receive power in dreams in which dead relatives appear. The Wintu shaman derives power from the ghosts of people, often of his dead children. The first indication that the Shasta have of shamanistic power is from dreams in which the ghosts of a dead mother, father, or an earlier ancestor appear. At least one Atsugewi shaman claims that shamanistic power is secured from ghosts. The foothill division of the Northern Maidu include ghosts of the dead among the spirits believed to be sources of shamans' power. Visits from dead relatives confer power also among the Yokuts. It is evident, then, that in northern California, and extending well into the central part of the state, a fairly solid block of tribes have the concept that shamanistic power is derived from ghosts. Moreover, this group is immediately adjacent to the Great Basin, where we have seen that a similar conception holds.[25] It is also suggestive that immediately to the east of the Shoshoni bands in the eastern Basin, the belief in ghosts as a source of shamanistic power appears among several of the tribes of the western Plains: Crow, Arapaho, and Gros Ventre.[26]

In northern California, among the Hupa, Yurok, Chimariko, and Shasta, we find the specialized concept of "pains" mentioned previously. These are looked upon both as the source of the shamans' powers and the cause of disease. The "pains" are thought to be animate and self-moving, sometimes with personality. They do not, however, possess human form or resemblance but are believed to be physically concrete.[27]

The shamans in other tribes of this region secure power from ghosts or other spirits, as we have seen, but among the Wintun groups, Yuki, Northern Maidu, Achomawi, and Atsugewi,

[24] Teit, *The Lillooet*, 287; *The Thompson Indians*, 354.

[25] Kroeber, *Handbook*, 63, 149, 514; Du Bois, *Wintu Ethnography*, 113 f.; Dixon, *Shasta*, 471; Park, *Atsugewi field notes*, ms.; Dixon, *Northern Maidu*, 269.

[26] Lowie, *Religion of the Crow Indians*, 380; Kroeber, *The Arapaho*, 451; *Ethnology of the Gros Ventre*, 276.

[27] Goddard, *Life and Culture of the Hupa*, 65 f.; Sapir, *Hupa ethnological notes*, ms.; Kroeber, *Handbook*, 63 f., 111, 852; Dixon, *Shasta*, 472 f.

"pains" are included among the causes of disease.[28] Certainly, here this belief is linked with the strongly emphasized conception of "pains" found among the neighboring groups. The disease-objects in other parts of California as well as in adjacent areas, sometimes designated as "pains" in the literature, are nothing more than a variety of intrusive objects commonly believed to cause disease.

The conception in northern California of the form of the "pains" is found to have important variations among the several tribes. The Hupa "pains" are of all colors; one looked like rough flesh; some were like crab, water-dog, arrow-point, or little deer. Those of the Chimariko are small double-pointed animal objects. The Axeki or "pains" sucked out by the Shasta shaman are described as being like a tiny icicle, spindle-shaped and sharp at both ends. When removed from the patient the "pain" can be broken to cause its owner's death, it may be softened in water and burnt in the embers of a fire, or it may be pushed into the river and drowned. The Atsugewi "pains" are either small needle-like objects or worm-like things that are animate, can propagate and talk. When extracted from the patient they can be made to tell who sent them to cause illness.[29]

The belief in "pains" is clearly a specialized concept restricted to a limited area in California. It is not known to the Paviotso nor has it been reported for their close dialectal relatives and neighbors, the Paiute of Surprise Valley, Mono Lake, and Owens Valley. Further, there is no evidence that a belief in this type of "pains" is known elsewhere in the Great Basin or in the Plateau area.

It will suffice to note that the association of this conception of the source of shamanistic power with the unique characteristics of the Californian control dances, through which the novice shaman inures his body to the presence of the "pains" and establishes control over them, centers in northwestern California among the Yurok and Hupa. Kroeber has pointed out that these features are most highly developed in this center. From these tribes the control

<hr />

[28] Kroeber, *Handbook*, 361, 197; Du Bois, *Wintu Ethnography*, 112; Dixon, *Northern Maidu*, 268, 280; Angulo, *Psychologie religieuse*, 562; Park, *Atsugewi field notes*, ms.

[29] Sapir, *Hupa ethnological notes*, ms.; Kroeber, *Handbook*, 111; Dixon, *Shasta*, 474, 488; Park, *Atsugewi field notes*, ms.

dances spread out gradually, diminishing in complexity and losing more and more elements, as far as the Maidu. In a re-examination and further analysis of the data, Spier has established the probability of the connection of the control dance of northern California with the tutelage of novices in the Kuksu complex centering further south in California.[30]

In south central California we meet again with the belief that animal spirits and natural phenomena are sources of shamans' powers. This is clearly the case with the Yokuts and Western Mono.[31] For the tribes participating in the Kuksu Society complex,[32] information is less definite, but it seems that supernatural spirits are not characteristically the source of shamanistic power. Curing ability is frequently purchased or the necessary outfit is inherited. As Kroeber remarks, shamanistic power is primarily a "matter of knowledge rather than experience." The only tribe in this area among whom shamans are reported to derive shamanistic power from spirits of water-holes, land, water, mountains, and sky, is the hill Patwin.[33]

Information is vague or entirely lacking for most of southern California. From the available data it appears that animal spirits play a rôle in giving shamanistic powers. Among the Desert Cahuilla, shamans are supposed to derive their power from Mukat, the creator, but the power is conferred through the medium of guardian spirits. These are probably the animals, such as owl, fox, coyote, bear, and others, that act as messengers to shamans. Powers noted for the Pass Cahuilla include bugs, humming-bird, coyote and bear. There is one Luiseño statement that shamans receive songs in their dreams from a rock, a mountain, or a person.[34]

With many of the southern California tribes, animal spirits appear in dreams which are induced by the narcotic jimson weed. Here, however, the spirits seem to be related more to the initiation

---

[30] Kroeber, *Handbook*, 852–853; Spier, *Klamath Ethnography*, 262–265.

[31] Kroeber, *Handbook*, 513; Gayton, *Yokuts-Mono Chiefs and Shamans*, 388; Gifford, *The Northfork Mono*, 49.

[32] Kroeber in a recent discussion re-defined and further delimited the Kuksu system. *The Patwin and their Neighbors*, 391 f. The distribution of the Kuksu cult (map p. 393) is reduced by about half that assigned to it in the *Handbook* (plate 74).

[33] Kroeber, *The Patwin and their Neighbors*, 292, 342; Loeb, *Pomo Folkways*, 320.

[34] Hooper, *The Cahuilla Indians*, 334, 337; Strong, *Aboriginal Society*, 115; Park, *Cahuilla field notes*, ms.; Kroeber, *Handbook*, 681.

rites than to shamanism. The Kawaiisu, Luiseño, Juaneño, and Gabrielino initiates expect to see animals which act as protectors in adult life; but there is a suggestion that the shaman also is given power by animal spirits. At any rate, with these people and the Northern and Southern Diegueño, the Cocopa, and the Akwa'ala of Lower California, securing shamanistic power is associated with the initiation ceremonies, and the emphasis in these rites is on experiences resulting from taking the jimson weed.[35]

The Yumans of the Colorado River present a somewhat different, but also specialized, concept. The Mohave and Yuma hold the belief that all power comes from the great mythological beings. The Mohave shaman, for example, insists that he received his powers from Mastamho at the beginning of the world. As we have seen, a similar belief is current among the Cahuilla. Animal spirits as a source of power, nevertheless, appear in this elaborately formulated conception of experience with the supernatural world in dream life. The Yuma obtain supernatural power both from animals and from mythical beings, but it appears that the number of shamans' spirits is rather small. The Cocopa derive power from nature spirits and animals that appear in dreams as human beings. From their animal names it is recognized in native thought that these spirits are animals.[36] The connection between the localized emphasis on dreams and the acquisition of shamanistic power will be considered below.

In surveying the situation to the east among the non-pueblo tribes in the western part of the Southwest, we find that notions similar to Yuma-Cocopa beliefs obtain, at least in part. The Havasupai sources of power are limited in number and are sometimes specified as animal spirits. Among the Walapai, the shaman is visited by the spirit of a dead relative, or power is secured from some geographical feature, usually a mountain. Animal spirits are not mentioned here. The Maricopa derive shamanistic power from animal spirits such as eagle, buzzard, coyote, horned owl. It is specifically stated that the number of spirits seems to be definitely limited. Ghosts are not mentioned as sources of power. The Papa-

[35] Kroeber, *Handbook*, 604, 640 f., 712 f.; Gifford, *The Cocopa*, 305 f.; Gifford and Lowie, *Akwa'ala*, 344 f.

[36] Kroeber, *Handbook*, 754 f.; Forde, *Yuma Indians*, 182; Densmore, *Yuman and Yaqui Music*, 101 f.; Gifford, *The Cocopa*, 309.

go shamans were given power by animals, and also apparently by ghosts of the dead. There is a suggestion that the songs which belong to the Pima shaman's power are derived from animals.[37]

Southern Californian conceptions of the source of power, along with those of the adjacent non-pueblo Southwest, are somewhat different in phrasing, and in certain instances distinct in content, from the Paviotso beliefs. Paviotso notions indicate relationships with the prevailing Plateau and Plains beliefs that a great array of spirits, both animals and natural phenomena, are potential sources of power. In the Plateau, development is along the lines of the number and variety of such spirits. The Paviotso, and possibly other Great Basin tribes, do not exhibit such a marked profusion of spirits, but the variety is appreciably greater, and the interpretation is different from that in southern California and the Southwest.

The Paviotso concept of dwarfs and ghosts as a source of supernatural aid for shamans reveals connections with northern California. These beliefs do not appear in the north among the Plateau tribes with the exception of the beliefs in water-dwarfs among the Klamath and Tenino and the Thompson conception of shamans deriving power from spirits of the dead. Such beliefs are not, of course, confined to the Basin and northern California; in the Plains, as we have seen, supernatural power is given by ghosts and dwarf-like beings.

The Paviotso notions, then, indicate in one instance cultural relationships to the east—with other Great Basin tribes and probably with the Plains; in other beliefs the connection lies to the north and east—with the southern Plateau and northern California. Therefore, in the several beliefs associated with securing power, different affiliations with surrounding areas are suggested.

Not infrequently in western North America we meet with a notion that there is a specialization of function among supernatural powers, i.e., certain spirits are sources of power which may be employed only for certain specific purposes. This appears in curative practices in connection with the belief that one spirit is more efficacious than others in treating a particular disease. There is little

---

[37] Spier, *Havasupai Ethnography*, 276 f.; *Yuman Tribes*, 249 f.; Kroeber, ed., *Walapai Ethnography*, 185 f.; Densmore, *Papago Music*, 82 f.; Russell, *The Pima Indians*, 261.

of this type of specialization among the Paviotso, but a suggestion of the notion is to be found in the statements that shamans with power from the rattlesnake can best treat snake-bites, those with power from ghosts are better able than others to cure sickness caused by ghosts, power from water-babies enables a shaman to treat effectively sickness for which they are responsible, and antelope-spirits give power for antelope-charming.

Information on specialization is lacking for the larger part of the Great Basin. On the eastern margin of the area among the Northern Shoshoni band of Seed Eaters, we find the association of certain animal spirits with specific diseases. The otter is invoked to relieve fevers, the bear only for open and bloody wounds, the woodpecker for venereal diseases. The eagle, on the other hand, is thought to give general curative powers. Similar notions of the efficacy of certain animals for particular ills prevail among the neighboring Shoshoni bands—the Salmon Eater and the White Knives.[38]

Among the Chemehuevi, three specialists, designated respectively as rattlesnake, arrow, and horse shamans, are regarded as having special powers to treat particular ailments or injuries. Still other Southern Paiute peoples recognize identical or nearly similar specialization of shamanistic function. In some instances at least, these types of specialization may be traced to the belief in differences in the potential ability of various powers.[39]

A more marked differentiation of function is evident in the northern Plateau. The Thompson recognize a definite group of spirits which give power only to shamans. There is a still larger class of spirits which act as guardian spirits indifferently for shamans, warriors, hunters, gamblers, and others. Similar beliefs seem to prevail among the Lillooet and the Shuswap. There is no evidence, however, that these people make any distinctions in the diseases which a particular guardian spirit enables a shaman to cure.[40]

The Sanpoil and Nespelem do not generally recognize specialization of function among the supernatural powers; yet some sha-

---

[38] Hoebel, *Shoshone Religion*, ms.; Harris, *Field notes*, ms.
[39] Kelly, *Chemehuevi Shamanism*, 129, 136 f.
[40] Teit, *The Thompson Indians*, 354 f.; *The Lillooet*, 283 f.; *The Shuswap*, 605 f.

mans gain reputations for the successful treatment of certain types of diseases or injuries. This is strongly reminiscent of Paviotso conditions.[41]

The Southern Okanagon shamans tend to recognize some specialization in their powers, although all shamans have some general curing ability. Supernatural powers gained for other purposes also show, to a certain extent, differentiation in the functions of spirits. Thus, coyote gives power for killing deer, the rattlesnake for treating bites, and so on. This type of specialization does not, however, seem to go very deep.[42]

Specialization in the function of powers of a somewhat different sort is found among the Warm Springs Tenino. Here the notion prevails that cures are dependent upon the strength and kind of shamanistic power. The first task of the curing shaman is to diagnose the cause of illness. Certain spirits such as thunder are of especial aid in this function. The diagnosis enables the shaman to determine whether he can cure the patient. Treatment will be successful only if he has among his spirit-helpers one that has a natural ascendancy over the intruding spirit. If, for example, an ailment is caused by the intrusion of the snake's spirit, the shaman can successfully cure only if he has a magpie, hawk or eagle among his guardian spirits, i.e., an animal or bird which in nature preys or is thought to prey upon snakes. This principle is said to prevail throughout shamanistic curing.[43]

There is little specialization of function of the powers recognized by the Klamath. Curing is possible only through certain spirits, whereas others enable the shaman to be clairvoyant. The Wishram exhibit even less tendency toward specialization of powers, although there is a marked difference in the potency of powers.[44]

There is little differentiation of function among the powers of the California tribes. The Shasta believe that the Axeki from the sun and certain stars are especially efficacious in all eye-trouble, and other "pains" have potency for specific cures. Atsugewi shamans control weather with power which they receive from the

[41] Ray, *The Sanpoil and Nespelem*, 201 f.
[42] Cline and others, *The Southern Okanagon*, ms.
[43] Murdock, *Tenino field notes*, ms.
[44] Spier, *Klamath Ethnography*, 103, 122 f.; Spier and Sapir, *Wishram Ethnography*, 237, 244 f.

clouds. Otherwise the shaman's function is dependent upon the amount of his power, not the kind. The powers received from the bear and the rattlesnake are the only two widely recognized specialized spirit-helpers in the state.[45] The conception that some powers are stronger than others, with somewhat different emphasis in certain localities, seems to be quite general in the Plateau, Great Basin, and California, and of course extends beyond this region to the surrounding areas.

The belief that shamanistic power is both beneficent and malevolent is found throughout western North America. Kroeber has remarked that central and southern California are a unit in regarding the shaman as having dual potentialities, either for causing death or for preventing it. This conception is by no means confined to California. Throughout the Plateau and, so far as evidence is available, generally in the Basin, shamanistic power is a source both of disease and the means of curing it. Only in northwestern California, as Kroeber notes, is this dual aspect of power less apparent. Even here the shaman, as among the Yurok and Hupa, may employ power to make people sick. On the other hand, among the Pomo curing and witchcraft seem almost totally separate. This differentiation apparently applies largely in the area where the Kuksu society is found. Turning east from this localized situation, we again meet the belief, among the Shasta, that the shaman's power, the Axeki, can be either the cause of illness or the source of power for its cure.[46] Except for the area of the Kuksu cult, the conception that supernatural power is at the same time to be used for harmful and beneficent purposes holds sway over all of western North America. That this dual aspect of shamans' powers is less apparent in northwestern California may be true, but it is no more than a matter of slight difference in emphasis and is not a distinction in the nature of powers, nor is there an absence here of the widespread conception of duality.

THE SHAMAN

The several aspects of the shaman's profession show striking differences in phrasing among the several tribes of western North

[45] Dixon, *The Shasta*, 486; Park, *Atsugewi field notes*, ms.; Kroeber, *Handbook*, 854.

[46] Kroeber, *Handbook*, 67, 853; Sapir, *Hupa ethnological notes*, ms.; Freeland, *Pomo Doctors*, 69; Dixon, *The Shasta*, 477.

America. The sex of shamans, distinctions between the shamans and the laity, specialization of function, and the position of the shaman in the social and political structure are all somewhat differently treated and weighted in various localities of the region under consideration. The distributions of these phases of the shamanistic complex will be examined separately.

The shaman's calling is open to both sexes among nearly all of the tribes west of the Rocky Mountains. As we have seen, the Paviotso have both men and women shamans, men, however, predominating in numbers. Although in theory female shamans can be as powerful and numerous as the men, in practice the tendency is for a greater number of men to acquire shamanistic power and usually those possessing the greatest power are also of this sex.

A very similar if not identical situation is found among most of the Great Basin and Plateau tribes. This is clearly the case for the Paiute of Owens Valley, Kaibab, Moapa, Northern Ute, Lemhi, Seed Eater, Salmon Eater, and White Knives bands of Shoshoni, the Thompson, Shuswap, Southern Okanagon, Sanpoil and Nespelem, Klallam, Wishram, Tenino, Klamath; and according to Spier's survey the same holds for the Quinalt, Snohomish, and Nisqually.[47]

It is reported that among the Nez Percé and Tillamook both sexes obtain shamanistic power. The Takelma shamans are said to be equally men and women. In the first two tribes men may predominate, and the Takelma case is not strikingly different from the prevailing conditions to the north. Only in the north among the Salish peoples of the lower Fraser River do we find an exception to Plateau-Basin situation. Information indicates that among the mainland HalkōmẽlEm, curing shamans are all men; sorcerers are both men and women.[48]

Conditions are radically different in northern California. The

[47] Steward, *Owens Valley Paiute*, 311 f.; Sapir, *Kaibab field notes*, ms.; Lowie, *Shoshonean Ethnography*, 291; Densmore, *Northern Ute Music*, 127; Lowie, *The Northern Shoshone*, 228; Hoebel, *Shoshone Religion*, ms.; Harris, *Field notes*, ms.; Teit, *The Thompson Indians*, 360; *The Shuswap*, 613; Cline and others, *The Southern Okanagon*, ms.; Ray, *The Sanpoil and Nespelem*, 200; Gunther, *Klallam Ethnography*, 298; Spier and Sapir, *Wishram Ethnography*, 107, 255; Murdock, *Tenino field notes*, ms.; Spier, *Klamath Ethnography*, 107–108, 255.

[48] Spinden, *The Nez Percé*, 256; Boas, *Notes on the Tillamook*, 6, 7; Sapir, *Religious Ideas of the Takelma Indians*, 41; Hill-Tout, *Ethnological Studies of the Mainland HalkōmẽlEm*, 361.

Yurok, Tolowa, Hupa, Wiyot, and Shasta shamans are predominantly women. Among the Hupa, only a few men were shamans, and only women are mentioned for the Yurok. Kroeber implies that the Chimariko shamans are also chiefly women. The Shasta shamans are likewise usually women, but male shamans are known, and appear to be more numerous in some sections than in others. The emphasis on female shamans extends to the Northern Maidu living in Big Meadows, where, according to Dixon, female shamans are more numerous than the male members of the profession. The numbers of men and women gifted with supernatural power seem to be about even among the Achomawi and Atsugewi.[49]

Among several of the tribes of northern California there is an unique association of "pains" as a source of power, the control dances, and the unusual feature of allocating the shaman's calling chiefly to women. These three appear together at least among the Hupa, Yurok, Chimariko, and Shasta. As might be expected, the distributions of the three traits do not coincide precisely. The concept of "pains" as a cause of disease, if not a source of power, extends somewhat beyond these four tribes; specifically to the Wiyot, Achomawi, Atsugewi, Wintu, Northern Maidu, possibly the Tolowa as well. However, with the Wiyot, Tolowa, and one of the Northern Maidu groups, women predominate as shamans, whereas among the Achomawi and Atsugewi the tendency for a greater proportion of women to acquire power is not so marked. There is, of course, no obvious connection among these three aspects of the shamanistic complex and, therefore, suggestive historical connections seem indicated. Satisfactory information on the Yana and Karok is lacking, but there are hints in the available data that these three traits may also be present in these groups as well.

Elsewhere in California, men predominate as shamans, but usually women also acquire power. This is definitely true of the Northern Maidu, exclusive of the Big Meadows group, Southern Maidu, Washo, Wintu, Yuki, Sinkyone, and Western Mono. There is,

---

[49] Kroeber, *Handbook*, 63 f., 111, 117; Du Bois, *Tolowa Notes*, 256; Sapir, *Hupa ethnological notes*, ms.; Dixon, *The Shasta*, 471; *The Northern Maidu*, 274; Angulo, *Psychologie religieuse*, 564; Park, *Atsugewi field notes*, ms.

on the other hand, specific mention that shamans are exclusively men among the Yokuts and Salinan.[50]

In the north central Californian area in which the Kuksu Society holds sway, information on the sex of shamans is not entirely clear. Both men and women "doctors," i. e., people who are able to cure by virtue of supernatural power, are found among the Northern Pomo, Huchnom, Wailakai, Wappo, and Coast Miwok. It is possible that male shamans predominate.[51]

The data concerning shamanism among southern California tribes are so meager as to make it impossible to be certain about the representation of women in shamanistic practice. The impression is given, however, that generally shamans are men. Strong specifically states that female shamans were not recorded for the Cahuilla and Cupeño. The only definite evidence of women as shamans is in the case of the Cocopa, among whom it is recorded that there are more male than female members of the profession. For the rest of southern California, shamanistic practices are probably almost entirely in the hands of men.[52]

The western non-pueblo tribes of the Southwest show no uniformity in respect to the shaman's sex. Among the Pima, medicine-men "who treat disease by pretended magic" are, in numbers, equally men and women. The "magicians," those who have power over crops, weather, and wars, are usually men. Mention is made of the admission of two women to this order. A third group which treats disease by a combination of supernatural power and herbal remedies includes both men and women. For the Maricopa, Spier states, "There is some question whether women were ever shamans." The Southeastern Yavapai recognize both male and female shamans, the men outnumbering the women, however. The Walapai shamans are of both sexes, although the number of women practitioners is small. The Havasupai state specifically that only men can be shamans.[53]

[50] Dixon, *The Northern Maidu*, 274; Kroeber, *The Valley Nisenan*, 274; Beals, *Ethnology of the Nisenan*, 385; Curtis, *The North American Indian*, Vol. XV, 97; Du Bois, *Wintu Ethnography*, 88; Kroeber, *Handbook*, 196; Nomland, *Sinkyone Notes*, 168; Gifford, *The Northfork Mono*, 50; Gayton, *Yokuts-Mono Chiefs and Shamans*, 389; Mason, *Ethnology of the Salinan Indians*, 183.

[51] Loeb, *The Western Kuksu Cult*, 9, 61, 83, 108, 114.

[52] Strong, *Aboriginal Society*, 64, 253; Gifford, *The Cocopa*, 310.

[53] Russell, *The Pima Indians*, 256–257; Spier, *Yuman Tribes*, 238; *Havasupai Ethnography*, 277; Gifford, *The Southeastern Yavapai*, 236; Kroeber, ed., *Walapai Ethnography*, 185.

The berdache or transvestite is not commonly a shaman among western tribes. No berdache among the Paviotso has ever been known to be a shaman. There is little information concerning the rest of the Great Basin, but it has been reported that berdaches do not become shamans among the Northern Paiute of Owens and Surprise valleys. From the available material it seems possible that this holds good throughout the area.[54]

Reports on Plateau cultures often fail to mention transvestites, but where we have rather full accounts of shamanism with no mention of such persons becoming shamans, we may assume with a fair degree of safety that the connection is lacking. Among the Wishram, berdaches are said definitely not to be shamans. Berdaches are, however, reported for the Klamath; a third of them became shamans. It should be noted, as Spier points out, that as both sexes are shamans, the transformation is hardly necessary for this purpose.[55]

Only with the Yurok, so far as information is available, is there a marked tendency for transvestites to become shamans. Kroeber estimates that, "one in every several hundred Yurok men on the average," underwent a transformation of sex. The native explanation given is that such men desire to become shamans. As the Yurok have male shamans, this as Kroeber indicates can be no more correct than the reason given by the Klamath. Apparently all the Yurok transvestites are shamans.[56]

Particulars are lacking for most of the remainder of the state, but several definite statements stand out in the literature. The Wintu berdaches, it is known, do not become shamans. Transvestites are reported for the Yuki, but nothing is said about their connection with shamanism. The Yokuts' men-women fulfill a special function unrelated to shamanistic practice; they prepare the dead for cremation or burial and in the mourning ceremonies conduct the singing and lead in the dancing. There is no reference to their becoming shamans. The Mohave have a special ceremony to induct youths into the transvestite condition. The only suggestion that the Mohave berdache might also be a shaman is contained in a reference to the variety of venereal disease that they

[54] Steward, *Owens Valley Paiute*, 311; Kelly, *Surprise Valley Paiute*, 159.
[55] Spier and Sapir, *The Wishram*, 221; Spier, *Klamath Ethnography*, 51–52.
[56] Kroeber, *Handbook*, 46.

treat. The Cocopa transvestite has no special function and none is reported to be a shaman.[57] Clearly, from the material available, sketchy as it is, there is, with the exception of the Yurok, no striking connection between transformation of sex and shamanistic power. Even if the Yurok conditions prove more widespread, let us say among the other tribes of northwestern California, sufficient evidence is at hand to indicate that the combination must be quite localized in distribution. Over most of western North America shamans are rarely, if ever, transvestites.

Throughout most of the Plateau area, the shaman is set off from other members of the group simply as one who has greater but not different power. With nearly all of these people, the majority seek and secure a supernatural guardian-helper. Accordingly, all or nearly all enjoy some supernatural aid. The shaman is differentiated largely by the amount of power that he possesses and the curative results which he is thereby enabled to obtain. To be sure, the Thompson shaman secures his powers from a particular group of spirits, but the distinction between shaman and laity is largely based on curing ability and practices rather than on the possession of unique power. Again with the Klamath, the shaman is one who has acquired more than usual power, although curing is possible only through certain spirits. As Spier points out, "This is a relative matter; some shamans have considerably more power than others, and everyone who has got power is in some degree capable of using it as a shaman does." This is also the western Plains view of the distinction (or lack of it) between the shaman and the rest of the group.[58]

The differentiation of shamans on the basis of the degree of power and curative ability holds sway from the north, among such tribes as the Thompson and Shuswap, southward into northeastern California at least as far as the Wintu and Atsugewi. The Achomawi and Atsugewi seek and secure power for every purpose, and the shaman is thus only one who has power sufficiently potent to enable him to cure. Supernatural experiences are had by most of the Wintu also. The same situation then holds here; the shaman

[57] Du Bois, *Wintu Ethnography*, 50; Kroeber, *Handbook*, 180, 497, 500, 748–749; Gifford, *The Cocopa*, 294.

[58] Spier, *Klamath Ethnography*, 107, 123; Lowie, *Religion of the Crow*, 344; Kroeber, *The Arapaho*, 419; Benedict, *The Vision in Plains Culture*, 10.

is distinguished from the lay person, not by the nature but by the strength of his supernatural experience.[59]

Although this is a fairly uniform conception throughout the Plateau, several exceptions are to be noted. Among the Takelma, guardian spirits are not for the usual run of people. The mass of people who are without power is designated by a special term, meaning "raw people." The Salish tribes on Puget Sound recognize two distinct types of power, those spirits that refer to the power of healing, given only to shamans, and those that help people gain riches by giving them luck in fishing, hunting, gambling, etc. Each kind of power is designated by a different term.[60]

In northern California, excluding the Wintu, Achomawi, and Atsugewi, the distinction between the shamans and the laity is more definitely marked. Among the Northern Maidu, Shasta, Hupa, Yurok, Sinkyone, and Tolowa, the shaman is sharply differentiated from the rest of the group through the possession of spirit helpers.[61]

In north central California, in the area of the Kuksu cult, shamanism is so heavily overlaid with the beliefs and rites of the secret societies that it is difficult to determine the nature and extent of local notions of the shaman's supernatural power. Loeb has suggested that guardian spirits do not obtain among the Pomo.[62] Certainly, in this area, those doctors who cure and the sorcerers who poison by invoking supernatural spirits are set off sharply from the laity as possessing different powers. In short, here the difference is one of kind rather than one based on the degree of power.

The information available for the central part of the state suggests that in this region the distinction between the shaman and the layman rests on the amount of power possessed by the shaman. This is clearly the case with the Yokuts, who state explicitly that the difference between the shaman's power and that of the non-professional is one of quantity rather than quality. Both men

[59] Spier, *Klamath Ethnography*, 250; Angulo, *Background of Religious Feeling*, 357; Park, *Atsugewi field notes*, ms.; Du Bois, *Wintu Ethnography*, 118.

[60] Sapir, *Religious Ideas of the Takelma Indians*, 42; Haeberlin, *SbEtEdáǫ*, 250.

[61] Dixon, *The Northern Maidu*, 267 f.; *The Shasta*, 472 f.; Sapir, *Hupa ethnological notes*, ms.; Kroeber, *Handbook*, 63 f.; Nomland, *Sinkyone Notes*, 168; Du Bois, *Tolowa Notes*, 256–257.

[62] Loeb, *Pomo Folkways*, 320.

and women acquire a little power for luck in hunting and gambling and for curing the simple illnesses of their friends and children. The shaman's power is but of greater quantity, resulting from a larger accumulation of dream-experiences. The great majority of the Western Mono likewise acquire guardian spirits. The shaman's spirit helper is regarded as more powerful than the guardian spirit of the ordinary person.[63]

The information for southern California is entirely too vague to allow us to be certain of the precise nature of the supernatural power acquired in the dreams induced by the jimson weed taken during the initiation rites of most of the tribes in this region. Further, we know nothing of how this power is related to or differentiated from the supernatural agencies invoked by the shamans in curative practices. There are suggestions that the Luiseño shaman dreams of "a rock, a mountain, a person, or something similar," and that in the Kawaiisu puberty rites there is an approximation to shamanistic experiences, but these references are so vague as to give us no clue to the distinctions, or lack of them, between the shaman and the laity.[64]

On the lower Colorado river, dreams are the sanctions for success in every kind of venture in life. Not only shamanistic cures, but bravery in war, luck in gambling, success in every special ability are all derived from dream-experiences. In spite of Kroeber, this special and peculiar phrasing of dream-life does not exclude the conception of guardian spirits. The Yuma, according to Forde's account, definitely believe that power is bestowed by an individual spirit, often of mythological beings, sometimes of animals. This is also true of the Cocopa, who derive power from dreams in which deities or spirits appear. Clearly, the peoples of the lower Colorado do not generally differentiate sharply between the powers of the shaman and the warrior, the gambler, or the singer.[65]

The situation is somewhat different with the Maricopa. The strong emphasis here on dream-experience for success in life is

[63] Gayton, *Yokuts-Mono Chiefs and Shamans*, 388–389; Gifford, *The Northfork Mono*, 38–39.

[64] Kroeber, *Handbook*, 604, 681.

[65] Kroeber, *Handbook*, 680–681, 754 f.; Forde, *Ethnography of the Yuma*, 181–184, 201–204; Gifford, *The Cocopa*, 303, 309.

similar to the conceptions of the peoples of the lower Colorado, but Maricopa dream-sanctions involve particular spirits. This establishes distinctions among those who have power. One spirit bestows the power to cure, another to sing, a third to bewitch, and so on. Moreover, although in theory power might come to anyone, only relatively few have power of any kind. Here, then, is a clear-cut distinction, not only between shamans and laity, but between shamans and others who possess supernatural power.[66]

Apparently with the Southeastern Yavapai, Walapai, and Havasupai, the shamans are differentiated from the rest of the people by virtue of their supernatural power. There is no indication that these peoples receive supernatural powers commonly for other than curative purposes. For the Havasupai, it is said that spirits are limited in numbers and are almost without exception the familiars of shamans.[67]

It is evident that the Paviotso do not fit neatly into any of these areas, for here, though in theory it seems possible for anyone to acquire power for different purposes—curing, hunting, or gambling—in thought and practice spirit-helpers are not had by the common run of folk, so that the shaman is decidedly set off from the rest of the group by virtue of his power to cure and cause disease. Only one who has been given by spirits the power to cure is designated by the term puhágəm. There seems to be no word for those few individuals who have powers for hunting, gambling, or warfare. Although these powers are of the same kind and are derived from the same sources, only the ability to cure gains for the possessor the title, puhágəm. Clearly, the Paviotso shaman is differentiated from the lay person by his curative practices; if not by virtue of special powers, at least by strongly emphasized functions. This view does not correspond closely to the shaman's distinction resting on degree or quantity of power that was found to be characteristic of the Plateau and parts of northern California, and in the central part of the state among the Yokuts and Western Mono. On the other hand, the Paviotso conception is even further removed from the Maricopa and Havasupai points of view. It may

[66] Spier, *Yuman Tribes*, 236 f.
[67] Gifford, *The Southeastern Yavapai*, 233, 241 f.; Kroeber, ed., *Walapai Ethnography*, 185 f.; Spier, *Havasupai Ethnography*, 276.

perhaps be said that the Paviotso theory seems to indicate a weakened form of the concept that power is available for all, with the shaman distinguished on the basis of greater quantity. This view is marked, moreover, by the strong emphasis on curative ability which further differentiates the practitioner from the layman. In this the Paviotso are not unique, but I believe that they have rather heavily stressed the curative aspect of supernatural power; and this in turn, in spite of theory, has led to a clear-cut differentiation between the shaman on the one hand, and the laity and the person with non-curing powers on the other.

It is doubtful that the Paviotso distinction between shamans and non-shamans holds for the entire Great Basin; but nothing is known on this point for most of the tribes in the area. Information is available from the eastern Shoshoni groups, where the situation is very similar to the Plateau and Plains. The Lemhi Shoshoni secure powers for invulnerability in warfare and for other purposes as well as to enable them to cure. There seem to be no sharp distinctions between the powers or the individuals upon whom they are conferred. Among the Seed Eaters (Shoshoni), practically every person possesses at least one spirit-helper. The distinction here lies in the source of power, as each spirit gives power for a specific purpose, one spirit giving protection in warfare, another the power to cure a certain disease, and so on.[68]

A somewhat similar notion prevails among the neighboring Salmon Eaters and the band known as the White Knives living to the westward in Nevada and bordering on the Paviotso in the vicinity of Winnemucca. These Shoshoni hold that each shaman derives power from several spirits—one confers power to cure a particular disease, another power to treat a different ailment. Invulnerability in battle and other non-curative abilities are derived likewise from spirits associated with specific functions. Here, as with the Paviotso, those who are regarded as the possessors of power for treating the sick by sucking out intrusive disease-objects or by restoring a lost soul are differentiated by a specific term. Those who treat the sick with prayer and herbs and those who are thought to possess supernatural ability in other lines are not accepted as puhagent (shamans).[69]

[68] Lowie, *The Northern Shoshone*, 224; Hoebel, *Shoshone Religion*, ms.
[69] Harris, *Field notes*, ms.

Several Shoshonean words for shaman are suggestive of at least a rather close linguistic connection. The Paviotso designation is puhágɔm; Owens Valley Paiute, pūhāga or púhùkù, Western Mono, puhake; Surprise Valley Paiute, puhágùm; Wind River, White Knives, and Salmon Eater Shoshoni, puhagant; Lemhi Shoshoni, búhagant; Seed Eaters, pɔhagant, Chemehuevi, puaxánt[i]. Allowing for differences in recording, it must be evident that this term is very similar in quite a number of groups. It is of further interest to note that in every tribe the term applies only to the curing shaman.[70]

Still another phase of shamanistic practice has to do with the distinction based on specialization of function. Among some of the tribes of western North America, certain shamans have the power to cure particular diseases or to perform other specialized functions such as controlling the weather or foretelling future events. Some of the aspects of shamanistic specialization have been mentioned in the previous discussion of the distinctions between various kinds of power and of the differentiation of the shamans from the laity. It will be profitable here to survey several additional aspects of shamanistic specialization and distinctions, particularly those not directly based on differences in type of power.

The Paviotso shamans, on the whole, recognize only minor distinctions in function. All shamans have general curative ability, but some tend to have greater success with certain types of disease or injuries than with others. Often reputations develop and a shaman comes to specialize in treating only those ailments for which his abilities are well known. This specialization seems to be largely a matter of public recognition; at any rate in theory it is rarely based on the possession of any particular kind of power. On the other hand, a suggestion of specialization appears in the opinions of some Paviotso that the shamans who derive powers from ghosts are more successful in curing the illness caused by these spirits, whereas those who receive supernatural aid from water-babies are more efficacious in relieving people afflicted by these beings; and the rattlesnake enables a practitioner to treat people bitten by that snake. As has been stated above, however, all who

[70] Steward, *Owens Valley Paiute*, 311; Gifford, *The Northfork Mono*, 49; Kelly, *Surprise Valley Paiute*, 189; *Chemehuevi Shamanism*, 129; Lowie, *Shoshonean Ethnography*, 296; *The Northern Shoshone*, 224; Harris, *Field notes*, ms.; Hoebel, *Shoshone Religion*, ms.

have these special therapeutic abilities possess general curing powers as well. Shamans with the power to control weather have also been mentioned, but commonly the elements are manipulated only to prove the shaman's control over supernatural forces. Probably the most clear-cut case of specialization is the antelope shaman, the person with antelope-power which enables him to charm the antelope in the communal drive. It seems that these people usually cure, in addition to their other duties, through the aid of the antelope-spirits or by means of other supernatural helpers possessed by the shaman. Finally, it may be recalled that the Paviotso make no distinction between the curing shaman and the sorcerer. The latter is conceived to have supernatural power which is not potentially different from that used for curing.

The Northern Paiute of Owens Valley recognize no specialization of any kind. Although one shaman who predicted storms is reported, weather shamans are said to be lacking. The Surprise Valley Paiute do not recognize specialization in their terminology, but there is a suggestion of distinctions among shamans; some are general practitioners, others confining their efforts to particular ailments such as wounds or rattlesnake-bites. Antelope shamans who charmed the animals for a drive closely resemble those of the neighboring Paviotso of Nevada. Shamanistic weather-control is reported, but nothing is said about a specialized function in that connection.[71]

Distinctions of another kind among shamans are reported for the Northern Ute. Two methods of treating the sick are recognized, and in each type there is a dependence upon supernatural aid. In one method, curing is dependent entirely upon the shaman's use of supernatural power; in the other the spirit-helper is invoked, but herbal remedies are also administered. It is not entirely clear, however, that this distinction is recognized in the terminology or even in the native thinking; it may only be so conceptualized in the account at hand, which is far from complete.[72]

A somewhat similar difference in the treatment of the sick is found among at least two of the Shoshoni bands, the White Knives and Salmon Eaters. These people recognize two types of practi-

[71] Steward, *Owens Valley Paiute*, 311; Kelly, *Surprise Valley Paiute*, 83 f., 189.
[72] Densmore, *Northern Ute Music*, 127 f.

tioners; the sucking doctors and those who have power to pray over the sick, to press and massage the patient, and to administer herbs. The distinction between these practices is terminologically recognized and only members of the former group can perform curing ceremonies. In addition to this differentiation, shamans in these bands derive powers from spirits with which special curative functions are associated. Another Shoshoni group, the Seed Eaters, recognize similar distinctions in the abilities of practitioners as a consequence of specialization in the source of supernatural power. Differentiation among shamans on this basis may occur in some of the neighboring groups such as the Lemhi, but information concerning them is lacking.[73]

Along with several other Southern Paiute bands, the Chemehuevi have certain specialized practitioners who treat such afflictions as injuries received in falls, snakebite, and injuries inflicted by horses. These distinctions in function are recognized in the terminology.[74]

The Plateau area is not a unit so far as shamanistic specialization is concerned. In some tribes, marked distinctions among shamans are current. In others there is relatively little differentiation of shamanistic function. The Thompson, Lillooet, and Shuswap recognize no marked differences among shamans. Sometimes shamans gain reputations for peculiarly successful cures, but this seems largely dependent on the quantity of their powers. Thompson and Lillooet shamans have become known for their ability to overcome the barrenness of women, but this has not resulted in a specialized practice. The Sanpoil, the Nespelem, and the Wishram also fail to recognize specialization of function among shamans. It is definitely stated that there are no weather shamans among the Sanpoil and Nespelem, and neither rattlesnake nor bear shamans among the Wishram. Klallam specialization rests on the reputations of shamans for particular kinds of cures. The Southern Okanagon differentiate in their terminology among the shamans who cure by sucking, those who treat illness by blowing, and those who blow and manipulate to relieve the patient. Further, as has been mentioned above, the powers of the Southern Okanagon sha-

[73] Harris, *Field notes*, ms.; Hoebel, *Shoshone Religion*, ms.
[74] Kelly, *Chemehuevi Shamanism*, 136–139.

mans are specialized, although all have general curing ability.[75]

There is yet another form of specialization among the Tenino which is reported to be even more important than the above. This is a marked distinction between war and curing shamans. The former are considered great warriors, as they are thought to be invulnerable. Such shamans practice weather-control and perform feats of legerdemain, but they never cure. On the other hand, war is tabu to the curing shamans, and these practitioners do not control the weather or engage in legerdemain.[76] From the available evidence, it would seem that Tenino forms of specialization are either unique or of definitely limited distribution. Clearly, these notions do not occur elsewhere in the Plateau, and as far as is now known, they are not present in the Basin.

The Salish tribes on Puget Sound, specifically the Snohomish, Puyallup, Squalli, Snuqualmi, Dwamish, Suquamish, recognize shamanistic specialization somewhat differently. A shamanistic ceremony of these peoples is performed by a number of shamans (usually eight) in concert in order to return the profane or non-shamanistic guardian spirit that has been lost. The practitioner who participates in these ceremonies must have a particular kind of shamanistic spirit-helper in order to visit the land of the dead and look for the lost guardian spirit. This is clearly a specialization of shamanistic practice, as it not only calls for a special spirit-helper, but it also involves a particular ceremony and has as its aim the cure of a single type of ailment. Moreover, it is exclusively the function of shamans who are sharply differentiated both from other practitioners and from the laity.[77]

The Salish of the lower Frazer river distinguish still different classes of shamans. Three types are recognized, those who cure by restoring the lost soul or by overcoming the effects of sorcery, those who cure injuries and wounds and interpret dreams and visions, and those who are sorcerers.[78]

The Takelma have two types of shamans, differentiated by dis-

---

[75] Teit, *The Thompson Indians*, 303; *The Lillooet*, 287; *The Shuswap*, 612 f.; Ray, *The Sanpoil and Nespelem*, 201; Spier and Sapir, *Wishram Ethnography*, 244–245; Gunther, *Klallam Ethnography*, 298; Cline and others, *The Southern Okanagon*, ms.

[76] Murdock, *Tenino field notes*, ms.

[77] Haeberlin, *SBeTeDA'2*, 249 f.

[78] Hill-Tout, *Ethnological Studies of the Mainland HalkōmēlEm*, 361, 364.

tinct practices and terms. One class of shamans can both cure and cause disease. The other class can cure, but members of this group are unable to inflict sickness on people. Shamans of the first class dance and use interpreters in curative practices; the others do not.[79]

The Klamath do not recognize specialized types of shamans. It is certain that weather, bear, and rattlesnake shamans are unknown. That curing is possible only through certain spirits has been mentioned before, but this has not developed into differentiation of function for particular diseases.[80]

Shamanistic specialization seems to be more widely and continuously distributed in California. Over a large part of the state three types of specialists are found: the weather, bear, and rattlesnake shamans. As Kroeber has pointed out, the greatest development of the idea of weather-control occurs in the south-central and southern parts of the state. The conception of the bear shaman, which he has neatly summarized, is known over most of the state from the Shasta to the Diegueño. The concept of the rattlesnake shaman, who both cures and prevents the bites of that snake, has its highest development with the Yokuts, who have a rather elaborate ceremony to protect the community from snake-bites. These specialized shamans are not so prominent among the tribes in the northern part of the state, although the Shasta have both rattlesnake and bear shamans.[81] This characteristically Californian type of specialization of shamanistic function, as we have seen, is entirely unknown to the Paviotso.

Among the western non-pueblo peoples of the Southwest, though several kinds of distinctions are recognized among shamans, specializations of the California type are not so clear-cut. The Maricopa conception is best described in Spier's words: "Professional segmentation among those having power was marked. These individuals were set off from one another by the possession of discrete powers from particular spirits. Thus Coyote and Buzzard gave power to cure, Eagle power to sing, Mocking Bird to orate, Frog to bewitch. The differentiation was not a quantitative

[79] Sapir, *Religious Ideas of the Takelma Indians*, 44.
[80] Spier, *Klamath Ethnography*, 108, 123.
[81] Kroeber, *Handbook*, 504 f., 854–855; Dixon, *The Shasta*, 484.

one in the sense of some having more power, of having dreamed of more spirits, although this may have been true of shamans who cured." Ordinarily a shaman knows the cure for only one disease; rarely does he know two or three. The non-curative powers include clairvoyance, bewitching, legerdemain, rain-making, and singing.[82]

The Pima distinguish three classes of shamans: those who treat disease by means of supernatural power, those who have power over the crops, weather, and power for war, and those who use a combination of simple remedies and supernatural powers in cures. These classes are differentiated by distinct practices, dissimilar ways of acquiring powers, and by separate designations.[83]

Weather and bear shamans are unknown to the Southeastern Yavapai, but doctors who are given power by the rattlesnake treat snake-bites. Other shamans are given supernatural power by a god. On the other hand, the Walapai have neither rattlesnake nor bear shamans. In fact, there is practically no specialization of shamanistic function in the latter group.[84] Turning to the Havasupai, we find three types of shamans distinguished. There are those who cure, the weather-shamans, and the practitioners who specialize in treating fractures, wounds, or snake-bites, or in following the deer. Several of these specialized activities in the third category are clearly reminiscent of Chemehuevi practices. It is said that all shamans dream, but those belonging to the first group have familiar spirits. The three types are not entirely distinct, as one man may have the power or the knowledge to perform two or even all of the functions.[85]

The position of the shaman in the social structure is of considerable importance in assessing the local variants of the shamanistic complex, especially since the social position or the influence of the shaman may point toward historical connections by virtue of clear-cut similarity in a number of tribes. Unfortunately, we know almost nothing about the rôle of the shaman in the social systems of the greater number of tribes in the Plateau, Great Basin, and

[82] Spier, *Yuman Tribes*, 238, 251, 285.

[83] Russell, *The Pima Indians*, 256 f.

[84] Gifford, *The Southeastern Yavapai*, 234–235, 239, 241; Kroeber, ed., *Walapai Ethnography*, 185.

[85] Spier, *Havasupai Ethnography*, 277; Kelly, *Chemehuevi Shamanism*, 137–138.

California. Usually the shaman has been studied entirely from the point of view of his rôle in the religious life. As a result, his participation in other phases of the cultural life has largely been ignored, or has emerged only as a by-product of the investigator's preoccupation with religion. Consequently, material comparable to that provided by Gayton's unrivalled study of the interacting rôles of chiefs and shamans in the social structure and life of the Yokuts and Western Mono[86] is to date non-existent. In spite of the handicap imposed by scant data, I shall attempt to indicate the range of difference, or the degree of similarity, in the position of shamans among the tribes for which information is available.

The importance of the Paviotso shaman in the political organization is not entirely clear Enough is known, however, to be certain that shamans are very influential in every aspect of the political and social life Many of the chiefs in the past have been shamans, though shamanistic powers are not necessary qualifications for political office Even those shamans of either sex who do not become chiefs often attain considerable prestige and exercise influence in the band. Shamans cannot be said to overshadow the chiefs, for, as we have seen, one man may perform both functions, but from the points of view of influence and honor, those who possess power can be said to rank favorably with the outstanding members of the tribe.

It must be evident from the foregoing that prestige and status are expressions of individual accomplishment, the result of personality and ability. Consequently, no valid statement can be formulated that will appraise in general terms the social importance of shamans in Paviotso society. One shaman may be respected by the entire group and consulted on a variety of problems involving personal affairs or matters of importance to the group, another may be merely a practitioner who is more or less successful in treating the illnesses of members of the tribe.

Almost nothing is known of the position and the rôles of shamans in the social life of other Great Basin tribes. It is said that the shamans of the Owens Valley Paiute, though influential, are rarely chiefs.[87] In spite of the lack of explicit information for the

[86] Gayton, *Yokuts-Mono Chiefs and Shamans.*
[87] Steward, *Owens Valley Paiute*, 304.

conditions in most of the Basin, it is safe to say that the shaman undoubtedly is an influential and important figure throughout this area.

Among the Plateau tribes, shamans are rarely chiefs, but they frequently attain positions of respect and influence. In the northern part of the area, shamans do not seem to outrank chiefs in importance. Nevertheless, shamans have authority and are leaders in ceremonial activities. This is clearly the situation with the Tahltan, Thompson, Lillooet, Shuswap, Southern Okanagon, Sanpoil and Nespelem, Klallam, Wishram and Nez Percé. With the Sanpoil and Nespelem a shaman, either male or female, is a figure of importance in the community, for the prestige of a successful practitioner is greater than that of an ordinary chief. Moreover, shamans have greater wealth than even the chiefs, who attempt to ingratiate themselves by frequently giving presents to those who control supernatural power. The Wishram shaman and his family occupy an exceptional position in society similar to that of the war-chief. Neither the shaman nor his family is likely to be molested, as the shaman's powers are greatly feared. Among the Klallam, the shaman is not so important socially as the chief and his family, but he is always respected and feared.[88] The shaman is likewise an outstanding figure in Klamath society. Here he is said to outrank easily the chief in importance. Apparently chiefs have relatively little power and influence, whereas the shaman enjoys considerable influence over his fellow tribesmen.[89]

There is almost no information on the social position of the shaman in the tribes of Northern California. It would be especially valuable to know the rôle of shamans in the social scheme of those tribes where women predominate in acquiring and exercising curative powers. Among the Hupa and Yurok, we know that the shamans are not the only religious functionaries, since the performance of world-renewing ceremonies, in which the recitation by an old man of long esoteric formulae figures prominently, certainly outranks shamanism in the religious life.[90] The relationship of the

---

[88] Emmons, *The Tahltan Indians*, 29; Teit, *The Thompson Indians*, 289; *The Lillooet*, 255; *The Shuswap*, 569 f.; Cline and others, *The Southern Okanagon*, ms.; Ray, *The Sanpoil and Nespelem*, 200; Gunther, *Klallam Ethnography*, 297; Spier and Sapir, *Wishram Ethnography*, 211, 247; Spinden, *The Nez Percé*, 256.

[89] Spier, *Klamath Ethnography*, 94.

[90] Goddard, *Life and Culture of the Hupa*, 82 f.; Kroeber, *Handbook*, 53 f.

priests, or ceremonial leaders, to the female shamans and the position of both priest and shaman in the society are aspects of these cultures that call for investigation.

Among the Shasta, where shamans are likewise chiefly women, the practitioners enjoy a high status in the community. Unlike the situation in the northwestern part of the state, the ceremonies performed by the shamans constitute almost the entire ritual acts of the Shasta. In spite of the prominence and influence of the female shamans, women never become chiefs.[91]

In north central California, the region in which the Kuksu cult flourishes, shamans and shamanistic performances are overshadowed by the rituals of the secret societies. As has been noted, both Kroeber and Loeb have discussed the possible underlying shamanistic basis of this cult, but the social position of shamans in these groups is far from clear.[92]

The shaman is easily the outstanding individual in Northern Maidu society. Shamans have great social influence; as a rule they are obeyed much more than the chief and are regarded with considerable awe. In addition to these intangibles of social and political influence, the shamans occupy a position of definite importance and leadership in the ceremonial life. Generally they are in charge of the burning-ground where the mourning ceremonies are held, and play a leading rôle in the rites which occur there annually. Shamans also function as leaders and directors in the ceremonial dances that figure prominently in the religious and social life of the Northern Maidu.[93]

The Wintu shamans were similarly important in both religious and social affairs. The manifold rôles of the shamans have been summarized by Du Bois: "In their [the shamans'] hands lay the transmission and molding of speculative thought. Their reputation of knowing all that transpired may well have exerted a deterring influence on the commission of crimes and the practices of witchcraft. They were called upon to predict the outcome of hunts, to restrain inclement weather, and in many different ways were allowed to direct and shape social undertakings. Their opportuni-

[91] Dixon, *The Shasta*, 451, 471.

[92] Kroeber, *Handbook*, 373, 859; *The Patwin and Their Neighbors*, 342 f.; Loeb, *Pomo Folkways*, 355, 366, 402.

[93] Dixon, *The Northern Maidu*, 246 f.; 267, 283 f.

ties were second only to those of chiefs, if indeed they did not sur-
pass them. The hold of shamanism upon the Wintu in comparison
to that of chieftaincy may be revealed in the fact that today shamanism still flourishes and has adapted itself to the impact of
eighty years of European contacts, whereas chieftaincy has disappeared and has been definitely rejected by persons themselves
entitled to the rank."[94]

In theory, the chiefs among the Yokuts and Western Mono are
heads of the political units, whereas shamans are not recognized
as officials but as professional doctors. However, we know from
Gayton's study, mentioned above, that the chiefs and shamans
play interacting rôles in the social life. The shaman has a certain
position by virtue of his curative powers, but in addition the
wealth and power of both chiefs and shamans are increased by a
system of reciprocal services. In every tribe a powerful shaman is
the close friend and associate of the chief. This alliance increases
the wealth of the chief and protects the shaman from the vengeance of those whom he has harmed, or is thought to have
harmed, by witchcraft. Shamans, then, in these tribes are not
alone possessors of supernatural power and professional practitioners, but they have also a well-defined social and economic
position associated with certain privileges and obligations.[95] Despite the paucity of material for the Basin and Plateau, the Mono-
Yokuts' situation unquestionably presents a picture entirely different from that of the neighboring areas, where the position and
prestige of the shaman are largely dependent upon the expression
of individual abilities.

Almost nothing is known of the shaman's position in the southern Californian tribes. Apparently among some of these peoples,
the shamans play an important rôle in the toloache ceremony, the
initiation rites in which jimson weed is taken. This is true, at
least, for the Southern Diegueño, Luiseño, and Serrano. Among
the Cocopa the situation is somewhat different, for although the
shamans administer the jimson weed decoction to boys who desire
a vision, this event is independent of the initiation rites.[96]

[94] Du Bois, *Wintu Ethnography*, 118.
[95] Gayton, *Yokuts-Mono Chiefs and Shamans*, 398 f.
[96] Spier, *Southern Diegueño Customs*, 318; Du Bois, *Religion of the Luiseño Indians*, 78;
Benedict, *A Brief Sketch of Serrano Culture*, 383; Gifford, *The Cocopa*, 303, 305.

The Mohave and Yuma have tribal heads or chiefs, but the true leaders are the war chiefs and the doctors, both of whom obtain their powers individually through dreaming. Kroeber has commented on the dangerous position of the shaman among the Mohave. Apparently the shaman's power of witchcraft is greatly feared by the Mohave, and they retaliate by killing shamans frequently. Nevertheless, Mohave and Yuma shamans unquestionably attain a position of leadership and exert considerable influence over their fellow men.[97]

Similar conditions prevail with the Maricopa and Halchidhoma. These people have chiefs whose positions are hereditary and whose authority is vague, but shamans and other dreamers are mentioned frequently as important in social life. It seems that shamans are, at least, equally prominent socially as chiefs and share the respect of the group with song and dance leaders, war-leaders, orators, and others who dream.[98]

It is said that members of the two classes of shamans, those who treat sickness with supernatural power and those who have power over the crops and weather and for war, are the most powerful and influential people among the Pima. These shamans are said to have even greater prestige than the chiefs.[99]

The Havasupai and Walapai shamans are also apparently held in high esteem, and through their personal qualifications may attain considerable influence and power. There is no indication, however, that shamans among these people become chiefs, for their functions are primarily curative. Whatever prestige and influence may reward their activities, they do not receive official political titles.[100]

This survey of the social position of the shaman will serve to show that the Paviotso, with most of the tribes of western North America, constitute a unit in according the shaman a place of prominence in the group. No doubt the shaman's status among many peoples is due almost as much to the fear of his powers as to respect and awe felt for his powers. It is also generally true that among the tribes of this region the shaman's position is not

[97] Kroeber, *Handbook*, 745, 778; Forde, *Ethnography of the Yuma Indians*, 133 f.
[98] Spier, *Yuman Tribes*, 154–155.
[99] Russell, *The Pima Indians*, 256.
[100] Spier, *Havasupai Ethnography*, 235 f., 280; Kroeber, ed., *Walapai Ethnography*, 185.

very definitely formalized. The extent of his influence, prestige, and his standing in relationship to the laymen of the society, is thus not dependent solely upon his possession of curative powers, but is often to a marked degree the result of other socially acceptable traits of personality, so that an individual can frequently reach a position of prominence through outstanding personal abilities and achievements, as where one shaman in a particular tribe may excel his fellow practitioners in certain accomplishments and as a result enjoy far greater respect, honor, and even wealth than his competitors. Clearly, throughout this area, with but few exceptions, the social rewards for approved use of supernatural powers are informally but emphatically recognized. The Paviotso seem to differ only in frequently combining political offices with the functions of the shaman.

The prestige and high status enjoyed by the shamans over most of western North America are not necessarily evidence of historical connection. The generalized social position of the shaman is variously interpreted in several localized areas, as we have seen. Thus the Paviotso attitude appears to be a local development; certainly it does not occur widely outside the Basin. Likewise the formalized reciprocal social and economic relationship of shamans and chiefs among the Yokuts and Mono has no parallel, so far as we know, in surrounding areas. These specific attitudes toward the social status of the shaman are clearly local developments which have as a basis the widespread generalized regard for the practitioner as an individual of considerable importance. That an appreciable measure of respect, awe, even fear should be accorded the one who is in possession of supernatual power is to be expected in cultures in which the bulk of religious thought and practice clusters around the acquisition and use of such power. Historical relationships will be indicated only when detailed information points to specific similarities in the way that the several cultures look upon the shaman's social status and formulate his obligations and privileges.

Acquiring Power

There are three widely recognized ways of acquiring super natural power in western North America: involuntary dreams, the vision quest, and inheritance. These three are by no means mutually exclusive, for in one tribe two or even three means of acquiring power may be practised. Nevertheless, the distributions of these practices do not coincide west of the Rocky Mountains. Certain aspects of these distributions have been exhaustively analyzed and defined by Spier,[101] and it will be unnecessary to duplicate his entire discussion here. It may be profitable, however, to consider Paviotso practices in their relationships to those of neighboring tribes. On the basis of this material, it may be possible to suggest the connection between Paviotso belief and practice in acquiring power and the related customs occurring widely in western North America.

It will be recalled that a Paviotso shaman acquires his supernatural power by dreams that come unsolicited, by inheritance from a dead relative, or by a visit to caves in the mountains. Inheritance of shamanistic powers is essentially nothing more than a somewhat special form of the customary procedure of securing power in dreams. Either the ghost of the dead relative or a spirit of the living kinsman appears in dreams and confers curing ability on the heir. If the ghost of a dead shaman initiates the bestowing of powers, the particular animal or other spirit from which the power is derived begins shortly to appear in the dreams. Inheritance follows no fixed line among the Paviotso, for any relative— brother, sister, son, daughter, nephew, etc.—may inherit the shaman's power. Again, the transfer through inheritance may skip a generation or two, or the power may be entirely lost. As far as the actual acquisition of shamanistic power is concerned, inheritance differs from involuntary dreams by the appearance in the dreams first of the ghost of the heir's dead relative, then by the actual appearance, in later experiences, of the spiritual source of power. This does not occur in all cases of inheritance, for in some instances only the source of power itself appears to the dreamer at the beginning of his experiences. The source of shamanistic power, or the spirit which confers it, is all that is inherited; none of the shaman's paraphernalia is retained by his heir.

[101] Spier, *Klamath Ethnography*, 247–259. The distributions of the quest and dream as sources of power in western North America are mapped on p. 251.

The Paviotso quest is quite simple. The person seeking shamanistic power, usually a man, stays in a cave for a single night. Fasting, purification, or other preparations are not necessary for the success of the quest. Moreover, no offerings are made, nor are such practices as running, diving in pools, and piling rocks employed to induce a power-vision. Power secured as a result of the quest is fixed in accordance with instructions received in later dreams that differ in no detail from the involuntary dream-experiences of those who acquire shamanistic power either by inheritance or through unsolicited experiences.

The conferring of shamanistic power in unsought dreams seems to be general in the Great Basin. Dreaming is the customary means of acquiring power by the Northern Paiute of Surprise and Owens valleys. Often these dreams begin in early childhood. The acquisition of power in dreams is also reported for at least three Southern Paiute bands, the Shivwits, the Kaibab, and the Chemehuevi. It may also be the means of securing power commonly practised among the other bands of this group. In former days the Southern Ute shaman generally received his power in dreams that did not involve fasting. The information on the four bands investigated by Opler is definite on this practice. Shamans acquire power in unsolicited dreams, and, as with the Paviotso, failure to accept the responsibility of the power conferred in this manner is to court sickness and death. Since the introduction of the Sun dance, about 1890, among the Utes of Utah, however, shamanistic power has been attained by participation in the rituals of this ceremony. Among the Northern Shoshoni band of Seed Eaters, spirits appear unsolicited and bestow power, or supernatural experiences can be sought in a lone vigil in the mountains. Unsolicited dreams may also occur among the Lemhi band, although Lowie states that "A man in quest of supernatural power would sometimes go up into the mountains at night." The White Knives and Salmon Eaters shamans secure power from unsolicited dreams, through inheritance, and by means of a quest. A striking similarity to Paviotso practices appears in the details of the quests of these three bands. Moreover, the dream-experiences by which power is actually conferred are substantially alike. The information for the Northern Ute, on the other hand, is not altogether clear. It is said that the little green men, referred to above, confer power on shamans. Densmore's informant said that he had first seen the dwarf when he was about twelve years old, and the little green man had appeared at intervals ever since that time. The curing songs were received when the shaman was in the mountains and fell asleep. The dwarf was then heard singing songs, which the shaman learned. This suggests a very simple quest along the lines of Paviotso and Shoshoni practices. It is at any rate clear that dreams are of fundamental importance in the acquisition of powers among the Northern Ute, for it is during such experiences that shamans first hear and sing aloud their songs. Cooke's recent field studies seem to indicate that involuntary dreams are likewise a source of power among the Northern Ute. Nothing is known of the acquisition of shamanistic power elsewhere in the Great Basin.[102]

Over most of the Plateau, power is secured in a voluntary quest for a vision. Since the quest is customarily open to all, guardian spirits are not restricted to shamans, nearly every individual having some supernatural power. Involuntary dreams in which power is bestowed are almost entirely unknown in the Northern Plateau. Moreover, this holds true for the tribes southward into Oregon, possibly as far as the Takelma. The exceptions to be noted are the Thompson, Shuswap, and Southern Okanagon. Among the Thompson, a few shamans inherit guardian spirits from parents who had been particularly powerful. These spirits appear unsolicited in dreams. In addition, among the Shuswap, some men inherit power from parents whose guardian spirits appear unsought in the heir's dreams, though this power is never so strong as that acquired in the quest. The Southern Okanagon recognize that power is inherited from dead relatives, but it is never sought, appearing first in dreams during sleep, Inherited power is in a special category here, for it comes regardless of the wishes of the dreamer and is attended by severe difficulty and peril. In all of these cases, the one who inherits power through involuntary

---

[102] Kelly, *Surprise Valley Paiute*, 190; Steward, *Owens Valley Paiute*, 312; Lowie, *Shoshonean Ethnography*, 291; *The Northern Shoshone*, 223; Opler, *Southern Ute field notes*, ms.; Hoebel, *Shoshone Religion*, ms.; Harris, *Field notes*, ms.; Densmore, *Northern Ute Music*, 128; Cooke, *Northern Ute notes*, ms.

dreams can, and often does, secure other guardian spirits in a vision quest.[103]

The combination of quest and dreaming among the Klamath, Modoc, Achomawi, Atsugewi, Northeastern Maidu, and Chimariko has been discussed by Spier. The Klamath case is typical. The seeker on the vision-quest does not obtain his power at the time, although he may be rewarded by a vision. Power comes later in dreams that are involuntary. This is strikingly similar to the Paviotso quest in which the promise of power is received in the vision; confirmation and the songs and other knowledge necessary for curative practice coming later in unsought dreams. The difference is to be found in the quest itself. That of the Klamath and other tribes is typical of the elaborate and extended exertions to secure visionary experiences found widespread in the Plateau.[104] The only exception known to these practices in the Plateau area is among the Tenino. In this group the child is sent on the spirit-quest to a lonely spot several miles from the village. He is expected to pile stones or tie knots in saplings as proof of his presence at the designated place. But the seeker of power does not run, dive, or swim in pools; and hemorrhages and trances are not experienced.[105] As has been noted, the Paviotso practice is substantially different from the general Plateau form of the quest, lacking as it does any of the features of the prolonged search for power involving physical discomfort and effort in diving, running, piling rocks and other violent attempts to invoke the desired vision.

In another phase of securing power, the Atsugewi align with the Northern Maidu. Some of the Atsugewi shamans first learn that power is to be bestowed on them when out walking, usually in the evening. This is an unsought experience. The Northern Maidu recognize as an alternative to the deliberate quest an involuntary waking vision in which power is acquired. Among the Northeastern Maidu, where the inheritance of shamanistic powers prevails, the dreams in which the numerous spirits' powers are bestowed are unsought.[106]

[103] Spier, *Klamath Ethnography*, 253; Teit, *The Thompson Indians*, 354; *The Shuswap*, 605; Cline and others, *The Southern Okanagon*, ms.

[104] Spier, *Klamath Ethnography*, 94 f., 254–255, 257 f.

[105] Murdock, *Tenino field notes*, ms.

[106] Park, *Atsugewi field notes*, ms.; Dixon, *The Northern Maidu*, 267, 275, 278.

The dreams of the Shasta shamans are somewhat different but are nevertheless involuntary. The first indication of power is from dreams followed later by a vision in which a voice is heard. The woman swoons and the Axeki come in the trance to teach her a song. Unsolicited dreams in which "pains" appear to bestow powers are also characteristic of the Yurok and Hupa. The specific content of the dreams differs widely. The Shasta candidate dreams of swarms of yellow-jackets or of some impending catastrophe, the Yurok of a dead person.[107]

Elsewhere in northern California, power is acquired in dreams, specifically among the Yuki, Sinkyone, Kato, Huchnom, Pomo, the hill Patwin, Southern Maidu (Nisenan), and Washo. In those tribes where the Kuksu Society holds sway, at least with the Yuki, Kato, Huchnom, Pomo, hill Patwin, and Southern Maidu, the shamans who secure powers in dreams are apart from those who acquire their status through initiation.[108]

In central California, information is available only for the Yokuts and Northfork Mono. The shamans of these two groups acquire power either in dreams, those of normal sleep during the night, or in sought visions.[109]

As the data stand now, among the tribes of southern California power comes to the shamans in dreams. This seems to be true of the Shoshonean groups in the southern part of the state as well as the Yumans of the lower Colorado. In fact in this region there is a strong emphasis on dream-experiences in contrast to the visions of the Plateau and neighboring tribes.

As we have seen, the spirits that appear in the dreams of this region are either animal or the mythological characters and gods. Sometimes dream-experiences are induced by taking the jimson weed, either as a part of the initiation rite or at other times. Certainly, the Kawaiisu, Luiseño, Juaneño, Southern Diegueño, Cocopa, possibly the Yuma, the Mohave, and the Akwa'ala of Lower California, use the jimson weed to provoke dreams in which various

[107] Dixon, *The Shasta*, 471–473; Kroeber, *Handbook*, 63 f.; Sapir, *Hupa ethnological notes*, ms.

[108] Kroeber, *Handbook*, 196; *The Patwin and Their Neighbors*, 292; Loeb, *The Western Kuksu Cult*, 38, 61; Nomland, *Sinkyone Notes*, 168; Freeland, *Pomo Doctors*, 58, 63–64; Beals, *Ethnology of the Nisenan*, 388; Curtis, *The North American Indian*, Vol. XV, 97.

[109] Kroeber, *Handbook*, 514; Gayton, *Yokuts-Mono Chiefs and Shamans*, 388; Gifford, *The Northfork Mono*, 49–50.

spirits appear and give power to the dreamer.[110] The Serrano shaman acquires power either from an involuntary dream or in the
initiation ceremony. The Serrano toloache rite in which a decoction of jimson weed is administered, is not a tribal initiation, for
only the sons of chiefs and priests, and all boys "who are different" go through the ceremony. Not all the boys who pass through
these rites become shamans. The Desert Cahuilla, on the other
hand, have the boys' ceremony, but the taking of jimson weed
has nothing to do with the acquisition of shamanistic powers.
Power is bestowed by the god Mukat through the medium of
guardian spirits which appear in unsought dreams.[111]

As Spier suggests,[112] the phrasing of the dreams may be mark-
edly different among the lower Colorado Yumans on the one hand
and the western southern Californians on the other. Without disregarding these differences, we see that this area is marked by
the emphasis on dream-experiences as the means of acquiring
power. The importance of the dreams, not the specific details
which are highly elaborated here, suggest the Paviotso case, in
which dreams are regarded as the most frequent way in which
power is bestowed. Both the quest and involuntary dreaming
are found in the Southwestern area. Spier and Benedict have
pointed out the presence among the several groups in this area of
the two means of acquiring power.[113] It will be necessary here only
to survey the western non-pueblo tribes in order to indicate any
evidence for affiliation with the Basin.

The Pima and Papago acquire shamanistic powers in dreams
which are not solicited by fasting or other unusual conditions.
As with the lower Colorado Yumans, dreaming for the Maricopa
is the source of all success in life. The dreams in which the powers
are conferred are stereotyped and almost wholly unpremeditated.
In contrast to this emphasis on dreaming, the Southeastern
Yavapai shamans receive power in trances. The trance-state in

[110] Kroeber, Handbook, 604, 640, 668 f., 680–681, 779; Spier, Southern Diegueño Customs, 312; Gifford, The Cocopa, 303, 305; Forde, Ethnography of the Yuma Indians, 205 f.;
Gifford and Lowie, The Akwa'ala, 344–345.

[111] Benedict, A Brief Sketch of Serrano Culture, 382–383; Hooper, The Cahuilla Indians,
334 f., 345–347.

[112] Spier, Klamath Ethnography, 252–253.

[113] Spier, Klamath Ethnography, 250, 252; Benedict, The Guardian Spirit in North
America, 36 f.

which the spirit or god bestows power seems to develop without a
quest or any other attempt to induce them. The Walapai and the
Havasupai shamans, on the other hand, acquire their powers in
dreams.[114] With the exception of the Yavapai, all of these tribes
have, in common with southern California and at least the western
Basin, dream-experience basic to the acquisition of shamanistic
powers.

A word should be said on the nature of the dream itself, although very little is known about this phase of experience with
the supernatural. Paviotso shamanistic dreams seem to be largely
auditory. This is at least true most frequently of the first power-
dream and of the initial phase of later dreams in which the spirits
instruct the shaman. The dreamer first hears his power coming;
often the spirit makes its approach known by singing. In some
cases, the power appears and otherwise makes its presence felt
in the later dreams of the shaman. With others, the experience
is at all times entirely auditory. There is no evidence that the
shamans' dreams follow any rigidly fixed pattern, but this may
be due to failure to investigate this point.

Unfortunately, little is known about the form and content of
shamanistic dreams in surrounding tribes. Although Spier has
clearly distinguished between the vision (the sensory experiences
which include hearing and seeing a spirit) and dreams (in our sense
of the word), in the ethnographic accounts the terms are often
used interchangeably, and their precise content and nature are
rarely described. The dreams of the lower Colorado Yumans are
best known. These dreams, as Kroeber points out, are cast in a
mythological mold; going back to mythical times, the shaman's
experiences begin with the origin of the world. The songs learned
in the dreams are put in the same form as the myths on which all
songs are based. In short, it is in a highly formalized and rigidly-
patterned dream-experience that the shaman secures his power.[115]

The Maricopa dreams also conform to a pattern; the experience
is thought to be an adventure of the dreamer during the night.

[114] Russell, *The Pima Indians*, 257; Densmore, *Papago Music*, 82, 84, 89, 102 f.; Spier,
Yuman Tribes, 236, 238, 244 f., 247; *Havasupai Ethnography*, 277–278; Gifford, *The Southeastern Yavapai*, 233 f., 239; Kroeber, ed., *Walapai Ethnography*, 185–186.
[115] Spier, *Klamath Ethnography*, 250; Kroeber, *Handbook*, 754 f., 775; Forde, *Ethnography of the Yuma Indians*, 201 f.

A spirit takes him from mountain to mountain, and at each place cures and songs are given to him. The dreams in which other powers are bestowed by spirits are similar in form.[116] Apparently the Walapai dreams do not follow a well-defined pattern, but, as with the Maricopa, travelling under the guidance of spirits is a usual feature in shamanistic dreams. These, like the Maricopa dreams, appear to be much richer in imagery than those of the Paviotso.[117]

We may expect to find important differences in the experiences encountered in the visions in contrast to those of dreams. These doubtless vary from tribe to tribe, but there may be significant basic similarities among several groups. The Paviotso visions secured in caves evidently stress the auditory element. Singing can be heard, and from voices and sounds spirits and animals are known to be near by. Only at the last does the visionary see a manifestation of supernatural power. The experiences of the seeker among the Paviotso and two Shoshoni bands, the White Knives and the Salmon Eaters, are identical in this auditory emphasis as well as being similar in an imposing number of other details, such as the attempts to frighten the suppliant, the appearance of a handsome man who confers power, and the likeness of the instructions received in the course of the vision.[118]

Chiefly auditory experiences seem likewise to characterize Southern Okanagon visions. Some never see their guardian spirits, either in animal or human form. Only the songs and instructions are heard. In any case, the auditory element at the time at which power is conferred is of the first importance.[119]

This and related aspects of the shamanistic complex, if better known, might throw light on some historical problems, for the details of similarities in dream and vision patterns may suggest important unsuspected cultural inter-relationships. The peculiarity among one or two groups in the Plateau of the appearance in human form of animal spirits during dream-experiences may be an illustration of this point. Detailed investigation might show that such a cultural patterning of dream-life is more common than

---

[116] Spier, *Yuman Tribes*, 247.
[117] Kroeber, ed., *Walapai Ethnography*, 230 f.
[118] Harris, *Field notes*, ms.
[119] Cline and others, *Southern Okanagon*, ms.

has been evident from the literature, and this would then illuminate something more of the history of this area.

It is not clear that manifestations of animal spirits in the shape of human beings are recognized by the Paviotso. Such may, however, be involved in the visionary appearance of a man during a search for power in a cave, a phenomenon, as we have seen, likewise reported for at least two of the Shoshoni bands. Possibly this conception is related to the Tenino and Southern Okanagon notion mentioned above of animal spirits assuming human form when they reveal themselves to an individual seeking power or in other shamanistic dream-experiences. At least the similarity is suggestive.[120]

The Paviotso quest for shamanistic power has been discussed above. Therefore it will suffice here to assess its position in relation to vision-seeking among neighboring tribes. As has been previously stated, the search for a vision in which power is acquired characterizes the entire Plateau area, as well as other regions of North America, especially the Plains. The Paviotso quest, however, bears little resemblance to the Plateau practice where the youth of either sex normally seek visions at puberty. This latter experience often entails extended efforts and privations, such as fasting, lonely vigils in the mountains, running, diving in pools or streams. The only exception noted to these customary practices is in the group noted above, the Tenino of Warm Springs. In comparison to these rigorous and protracted efforts, the Paviotso practice of visiting a cave for a single night is an extremely simplified version of the power-quest. There is still another significant difference in that among Plateau tribes nearly everyone seeks power in a vision. The first occasion is usually puberty, but often the quest is repeated in later life in order to renew and enhance power already gained or to acquire power for the first time. On the other hand, only a relatively small proportion of the Paviotso deliberately seek power, and these perhaps only after dream-experiences have suggested that power can be acquired. Again, there is no evidence that the Paviotso ever undertake the quest at puberty. Only mature men are known to have acquired power in this fashion.

[120] Murdock, *Tenino field notes*, ms.; Cline and others, *Southern Okanagon*, ms.

In an additional important feature, the Plateau quest differs radically from that practised by the Paviotso. Frequently, among people of the former area, with the Tenino again as an exception, the successful search for a vision is attended by violent physiological reactions—a trance state and often bleeding from the nose and mouth. None of these reactions is manifested by a Paviotso who is successful in his quest for power.

In another connection we have mentioned the simplified form of the power-quest among other Basin tribes. Specifically, this institution has been reported for the Surprise Valley Paiute, the Lemhi, Wind River, Seed Eater, Salmon Eater, and White Knives bands of Shoshoni, at least for the Chemehuevi band of the Southern Paiute, with a strong suggestion that the Northern Ute also seek powers in the mountains. In all of these tribes, the quest is similar to that practised by the Paviotso, a lonely vigil in the mountains unaccompanied by fasting, self-torture, or unusual and prolonged exertions. With the introduction of the Sun Dance among the Southern Ute, shamanistic power is sought by participation in the rites of this ceremony. But this quest differs essentially from that found elsewhere in the Basin. Information for other tribes in this area is entirely lacking; therefore it cannot be said definitely that the quest is either present or absent in large parts of the region.[121]

It must be evident, then, that the Paviotso quest, as well as that of neighboring Basin people, if historically related to the characteristic Plateau search for a power-vision, represents an extremely modified or very simple form of a typical Plateau complex. Further, the quest has not become the chief means of securing power for the Paviotso as it has to the north. It is of course apparent that the Basin adjoining the Plains, in which the quest figures prominently, may have derived elements from that region. But here again there are few definite points of similarity between practices in the two areas, for the distinctions between Plateau and Plains visions that have been pointed out by Benedict and Spier are also those that distinguish the Basin quest from Plains

[121] Kelly, *Surprise Valley Paiute*, 190; *Chemehuevi Shamanism*, 129; Lowie, *Shoshonean Ethnography*, 291, 295–296; *The Northern Shoshone*, 223–225; Hoebel, *Shoshone Religion*, ms.; Harris, *Field notes*, ms.; Densmore, *Northern Ute Music*, 128; Cooke, *Northern Ute Field Notes*, ms.

usages. Certainly among the Paviotso there is no inducement, as there is in the Plains, to seek supernatural aid for specific undertakings and occasions.[122] It seems evident, then, that whatever may be the historical source of the quest in the Basin, its simplicity and relative unimportance there indicate no significantly close linkage with these neighboring areas.

The quest for supernatural power is also practised in central and northern California. The combination of quest and dreaming has already been mentioned for the Northeastern Maidu, Achomawi, Atsugewi and Chimariko. The Western Mono, Yokuts, Wiyot and Sinkyone also deliberately undertake a quest for power. The shamans among the Shasta, Yurok, and Hupa acquire power in dreams, but non-curing power may be acquired through a quest.[123] The Wintu shamans secure power in an initiation ceremony which is quite distinct from the varieties of quests discussed above. This rite is held under the direction of the experienced shamans, and participation is entirely voluntary.[124]

The several features of the quest in California are not uniformly distributed. As might be expected, the Northern Maidu, Atsugewi, and Shasta seeking of power involves such customs as diving in pools, piling rocks, and other forms of strenuous effort, similar to the practices found to the north, as among the Klamath. But with the Shasta at least, this procedure is only for the acquisition of luck or power in hunting; shamanistic power, as we have seen, is acquired in an entirely different fashion. The Yokuts and Western Mono, on the other hand, have a much simpler form of power-seeking which is similar in several details to the Paviotso quest.

Securing shamanistic powers through a vision quest is not a southern Californian practice, for here the dream takes the place of the vision. In the adjacent Southwest, where dreams as a means of acquiring power also hold sway, the quest is either entirely lacking or of little importance. The Maricopa and the Walapai believe that it is possible to seek experience with spirits, but in both

[122] Benedict, *The Vision in Plains Culture*, 12 f.; Spier, *Klamath Ethnography*, 249–250.

[123] Dixon, *The Northern Maidu*, 279; *Notes on Achomawi and Atsugewi*, 216; *The Chimariko*, 303; *The Shasta*, 489; Park, *Atsugewi field notes*, ms.; Gifford, *The Northfork Mono*, 49 f.; Kroeber, *Handbook*, 68, 117, 513–514; Gayton, *Yokuts-Mono Chiefs and Shamans*, 388–389; Nomland, *Sinkyone Notes*, 168; Goddard, *Life and Culture of the Hupa*, 66.

[124] Du Bois, *Wintu Ethnography*, 88–90.

groups such practices are rarely followed. The Maricopa visit caves, in which candidates in a waking state are visited by spirits, but power is not conferred at this time. With the Walapai the infrequent quest takes place after dreaming has already started. The candidate then spends four nights in a cave communicating with the spirit of the mountains.[125] The quest has not been reported for other Yuman-speaking tribes, but it is clearly indicated by the available evidence that in this region vision-seeking is subordinated to acquiring power in dreams.

The inheritance of shamanistic power has been discussed for the Paviotso. It is the power, not the paraphernalia, that is transmitted to the heir. Further, there is nothing fixed in the line of descent. The power may go to any relative of the dead shaman or it may be lost. It should also be kept in mind that all such transmission of power is based directly on dreams, for the heir must undergo experiences similar to those of non-hereditary shamans.

There is no suggestion of inheritance for the Basin tribes to the east of the Paviotso, but data from these groups are too meager to exclude the possibility of this concept. The Northern Paiute of Owens valley hold that shamans' powers run in families.[126] At least in some cases, the Chemehuevi transmit shamans' songs and spirits from one generation to another. This appears to be unique among the Southern Paiute, for Kelly states, " . . . semi-inheritance of shamanistic power is a notion quite foreign to the Southern Paiute at large; it was encountered only among the two western-most groups, the Las Vegas and the Chemehuevi."[127]

The extension of power-inheritance in the Plateau has been surveyed by Spier. He has plausibly suggested also the relation of this concept to the tendency on the Northwest Coast to fix inheritance of experiences with ancestral guardian spirits.[128] It is necessary here only to note the occurrence of the hereditary transmission of shamanistic power among the Thompson, Shuswap, Southern Okanagon, Klallam, Nez Percé (the shaman's status is inherited here), Klamath, and Tenino. Spier adds Quinalt and Puget Sound Salish. Only with the Tenino is it clearly evident that

[125] Spier, *Yuman Tribes*, 244–245; Kroeber, ed., *Walapai Ethnography*, 186.
[126] Steward, *Owens Valley Paiute*, 311.
[127] Kelly, *Chemehuevi Shamanism*, 130–131.
[128] Spier, *Klamath Ethnography*, 247–249.

the majority of shamans inherit their spirits from a parent who was a practitioner.[129]

In northern California among the Shasta and Northeastern Maidu, inheritance is firmly fixed. In the Northeastern Maidu case, power is automatically transmitted from parent to child. Also with the Shasta, the shaman's position is for the most part hereditary.[130]

A tendency toward inheritance of powers, sometimes involving the belief that shamans run in families, is reported for the Hupa, Chimariko, Wintu and Western Mono.[131] With these peoples, the transmission of spirits is at the basis of inheritance, in contrast to the situation in which shamanistic status is acquired from the instruction of an older relative or the inheritance of paraphernalia, as among the Pomo, Nisenan (Southern Maidu) and valley Patwin.[132] As Spier points out, the inheritance of "outfits" and the instructing of the shamanistic successor affiliate with the initiation of members of the secret society in this area.[133]

There is no evidence that powers are inherited among any of the southern California tribes. So far, inheritance has been reported only for the Cocopa and Akwa'ala of Lower California, and the Pima, Maricopa, Walapai, and Havasupai. It is clear, however, that no strong emphasis is placed on hereditary transmission of powers among these groups for, as is the case elsewhere, the power is actually conferred in dreams.[134]

Inheritance among the Paviotso bears resemblances to the loose tendency to transmit power along family lines that is found, on the one hand, among some of the northern California tribes, and on the other, among the Southwestern peoples just mentioned. In the absence of more complete data, it is unprofitable to suggest

[129] Teit, *The Thompson Indians*, 354; *The Shuswap*, 605; Cline and others, *Southern Okanagon*, ms.; Gunther, *Klallam Ethnography*, 297; Spinden, *The Nez Percé*, 247, 256; Spier, *Klamath Ethnography*, 97, 247–248; Murdock, *Tenino field notes*, ms.

[130] Dixon, *The Northern Maidu*, 274–275; *The Shasta*, 471, 477.

[131] Sapir, *Hupa ethnological notes*, ms.; Dixon, *The Chimariko*, 303; Du Bois, *Wintu Ethnography*, 90 f.; Gifford, *The Northfork Mono*, 50.

[132] Kroeber, *The Patwin and their Neighbors*, 285; Freeland, *Pomo Doctors*, 59; Loeb, *Pomo Folkways*, 320; Beals, *Ethnology of the Nisenan*, 385 f.

[133] Spier, *Klamath Ethnography*, 249.

[134] Gifford, *The Cocopa*, 309; Gifford and Lowie, *Notes on the Akwa'ala*, 345; Spier, *Yuman Tribes*, 240–241; *Havasupai Ethnography*, 277–278; Russell, *The Pima Indians*, 256; Kroeber, ed., *Walapai Ethnography*, 185.

historical linkages of the Paviotso form of inheritance with either the tribes of the Southwest or with those of California. But it does seem evident that the Chemehuevi notions are strongly reminiscent of those of the Paviotso. Likewise, the Tenino formulation of the frequency of inheritance of power is suggestive of certain Paviotso beliefs, and bears as well distinct resemblances to the ideas current in several of the north central California groups. Suggestions of historical relations on the basis of similarity of concepts of inheritance await more definite data on this phase of shamanism in western North America.

The Curing Performance

The curative practices of the Paviotso shamans are on the whole simple rituals directed toward first diagnosing the patient's illness and then removing or overcoming those supernatural forces that are thought to be responsible. The curing performance consists of singing, in which the spectators join, dancing, which is little more than a few steps made around the fire by the shaman or an assistant, smoking, often a trance, and sucking. However simple these rites are, they constitute the chief religious ceremonies of the Paviotso. Moreover, as the curing performance is open to the public and food is served at an intermission, the occasion has a strong social appeal.

The special performances of novices in which control of the power is proved, and the shamanistic performances, often held in midwinter for the purpose of exhibiting power, are rites which are not practised by the Paviotso. Shamans are called upon to perform in public only for curing purposes and for the charming of antelope in a communal drive. The novice who has recently acquired power simply tells people of his ability to cure and then demonstrates his control of supernatural power when he is called upon to treat a patient. Failure in the first attempt does not necessarily exclude him from the ranks of the shamans, as he may be invited again to prove his curing powers.

Performances of the novices before they actually begin to cure, and public exhibitions of powers by other shamans have not been reported for any of the Basin tribes. This is the case specifically for the Northern Paiute of Owens and Surprise valleys, Shivwits,

Southern Ute, Northern Ute, Wind River, Lemhi and Seed Eater Shoshoni.[135] In view of the outstanding character of these performances and their importance in those cultures for which they have been reported, it is doubtful that they would have entirely escaped attention. The demonstration performances of novices and public exhibitions of shamans are known to many of the neighboring tribes, however. Both of these performances figure prominently in the ceremonial life of nearly all Plateau groups. Another type of dance for the novice, the performance in which control over spirits or powers is gained, is characteristic of many northern Californian neighbors of the Paviotso. The several types of novice dances and the winter shamanistic performances have been analyzed and their distributions surveyed by Spier.[136] It will suffice to note here that none of these public shamanistic performances so important in the rituals of tribes immediately to the east and north of the Paviotso, has reached these people nor apparently any of the other Great Basin groups.

Since details of the curing performances of many western tribes are lacking, it is frequently impossible to make specific comparisons with Paviotso practices. Nevertheless, it may be of some significance to survey the indicated similarities in the curative rites of several neighboring tribes. Throughout this region the general plan of procedure in curing seems to be much the same. The shaman is asked by members of the family to treat a patient, the fee is agreed upon, the shaman sings and smokes over the patient, dancing if it occurs at all is very simple, the cause of illness is diagnosed, and a disease object is removed or the soul of the patient is recovered and restored. These general practices obtain throughout the Plateau, most of northern and central California, with the Paviotso and their Basin neighbors about whom we have information, among the Yumans on the lower Colorado river and the adjacent Southwestern area. The differences in practice merely involve, on the whole, the details that are fitted into the general procedure in curing. Thus, the removal from the patient of an intrusive disease-object is accomplished primarily by sucking, so

[135] Steward, *Owens Valley Paiute*, 311 f.; Kelly, *Surprise Valley Paiute*, 189 f.; Lowie, *Shoshonean Ethnography*, 291 f.; *The Northern Shoshone*, 223 f.; Densmore, *Northern Ute Music*, 127 f.; Hoebel, *Shoshone Religion*, ms.
[136] Spier, *Klamath Ethnography*, 259–267.

far as we know positively, among the Southern Ute, Wind River, Lemhi, Seed Eater, White Knives, and Salmon Eater bands of the Shoshoni, Paviotso, Surprise Valley Paiute, Owens Valley Paiute, Chemehuevi, Western Mono, Yokuts, Southern Maidu, Northern Maidu, Atsugewi, Achomawi, Shasta, Wintu, Chimariko, Hupa, Yurok, Wiyot, Sinkyone, Yuki, Tolowa, Klamath, Tenino, Takelma, Klallam, and Southern Okanagon.[137] There are local differences in the preparations for the sucking as well as in the actual removal of the disease-object. The Klamath shaman, for example, bites the patient's body when he sucks, whereas the Paviotso shaman draws the intrusive object through the unbroken skin. It should be noted that the curing rites of the Shoshoni bands for which satisfactory material exists, show striking similarities to Paviotso practises. Thus, details of shamanistic curing among the White Knives and Salmon Eaters differ at only a few points from the account of the Paviotso rituals given above.[138]

Sucking is not the only method of removing the causes of disease in western North America. The Wishram, Sanpoil and Nespelem, Shuswap, coast Salish, and Kootenay draw out or drive away the intrusive object by songs and incantations, by spraying the patient's body, and by massage. Among some tribes, these practices vary with individual shamans; some suck, others draw out the object. This is true at least of the Thompson, Lillooet, and Southern Okanagon and is probably the case with other Plateau peoples.[139]

Sucking is practised among most of the Yuman tribes of southern California and the adjacent Southwest, specifically the Yuma,

[137] Lowie, *Shoshonean Ethnography*, 292, 296; *The Northern Shoshone*, 228; Hoebel, *Shoshone Religion*, ms.; Harris, *Field notes*, ms.; Kelly, *Surprise Valley Paiute*, 192; *Chemehuevi Shamanism*, 132; Steward, *Owens Valley Paiute*, 313; Gifford, *The Northfork Mono; Southern Maidu Ceremonies*, 243; Kroeber, *Handbook*, 66, 117, 197, 515; Beals, *Ethnology of the Nisenan*, 387; Dixon, *The Northern Maidu*, 270; *Some Shamans of Northern California*, 25; *The Shasta*, 478; *The Chimariko*, 303; Park, *Atsugewi field notes*, ms.; Du Bois, *Wintu Ethnography*, 104–106; *Tolowa Notes*, 257; Goddard, *Life and Culture of the Hupa*, 65; Nomland, *Sinkyone Notes*, 168; Spier, *Klamath Ethnography*, 126; Murdock, *Tenino field notes*, ms.; Sapir, *Religious Ideas of the Takelma*, 44; Gunther, *Klallam Ethnography*, 298; Cline and others, *The Southern Okanagon*, ms.

[138] Harris, *Field notes*, ms.

[139] Spier and Sapir, *Wishram Ethnography*, 246; Ray, *The Sanpoil and Nespelem*, 204; Teit, *The Shuswap*, 612; *The Thompson Indians*, 360 f.; *The Lillooet*, 287 f.; Hill-Tout, *Ethnological Studies of Mainland Halkōmē'lEm*, 361; Chamberlain, *Kootenay Medicine Men*, 97; Cline and others, *The Southern Okanagon*, ms.

Southern Diegueño, Cocopa, Maricopa, Southeastern Yavapai, Walapai, and Havasupai. Of the Mohave, Kroeber says, "There is no theory of disease-objects projected into human bodies. Hence the physician sucks little if at all." But this statement clearly does not hold true for most of the neighboring Yumans, who share with the Mohave other religious beliefs strongly colored by dream-experiences.[140]

Sucking in the curing rite does not necessarily indicate the belief that an intrusive object causes disease. The Maricopa shamans, as has been indicated, suck the patient, but the illness is believed to result from dreams. The shaman then sucks, "to take out the fever," not disease-objects.[141] How widespread this particular interpretation of the cause and cure of sickness is cannot be determined from the data available at present, but the conception of dreams as a cause of sickness to be removed by the shaman either through sucking or by other means is strikingly similar to Paviotso beliefs which are to be discussed below.

In addition to sucking, other techniques of treating illness are widely employed in western North America. The return of the patient's lost or stolen soul is a widespread shamanistic practice in this region. Often the shaman goes into a trance while his own spirit goes in search of the patient's soul and returns it in order to bring about recovery. From the information available, this practice seems to be fairly similar throughout the areas considered here. There are local differences in interpretation and of elaboration, but the analysis of these must await more detailed reporting.

As the ethnographic data now stand for most of the region west of the Rocky Mountains, the Great Basin, Plateau, California, and the adjacent non-pueblo tribes of the Southwest appear to be a unit so far as generalized curing practices are concerned. Unquestionably differences of genuine historical significance exist, but the scanty material does not offer satisfactory evidence of interareal connections beyond that contained in the suggestion of a fairly uniform generalized basis for the practices of this region as well as those in a large part of the rest of the continent. What-

[140] Forde, *The Yuma Indians*, 185; Spier, *Southern Diegueño Customs*, 313; *Yuman Tribes*, 283; *Havasupai Ethnography*, 279; Gifford, *The Cocopa*, 310; *The Southeastern Yavapai*, 234; Kroeber, ed., *Walapai Ethnography*, 187; Kroeber, *Handbook*, 775.
[141] Spier, *Yuman Tribes*, 280–281, 283.

ever the linkages that only a fuller record will make evident, this survey has at least suggested that on the whole the curing performance throughout this region is a simple rite performed usually by an individual shaman; the important exception is the previously noted performance of several shamans in a spirit-restoring ceremony among several coast Salish tribes. Another point of considerable historical significance that has been alluded to previously may again be mentioned in this connection. In the Plateau and northern California, the more elaborate shamanistic ceremonies appear in connection with spirit control, both in the rites for the novice and in the winter performances of shamans. Curing rites are not nearly so impressive as these performances; moreover, they lack elaboration of detail. In the Basin, probably generally, but at least with the Paviotso, the situation is otherwise. In the absence of other shamanistic performances, the emphasis is on the curative practices; and although these do not attain the complexity of the winter and novice ceremonies to the north, they are the center of attention in religious observance. Thus, although Basin shamanistic curing seems to reveal no greater elaboration than the practices of doctors in the Plateau and in northern California, far greater importance is attached to them by the Paviotso than is the case to the west and north. This contrast between the Great Basin on one hand and Plateau and northern California on the other is quite clear and definite. Although from the point of view of the Basin this distinction may be largely negative on the side of content, it has led to certain positive developments in the coloring of important attitudes towards disease and curing rites. Clearly, then, the Paviotso, and possibly the entire Basin, stand apart from the Plateau and California in several important particulars despite the evident fact that they share many practices closely associated with this aspect of the culture.

The Shaman's Speaker

In the curing performance, the Paviotso shaman is attended by a speaker who interprets for the spectators the rapid mumbled speech of the shaman. This assistant does not possess supernatural power. In addition to interpreting for the benefit of the spectators, the speaker leads the singing when the shaman is sucking or is otherwise employed. At the beginning of the performance he may also address the cause of sickness, telling it of the shaman's power or, during a pause in the curing, he may exhort the shaman to drive away the illness.

Little is known of the shaman's assistant elsewhere in the Great Basin. Steward reports that a famous Shoshoni shaman living in the mountains near the Panamint valley employed an assistant who explained the meanings of the words in the songs. This doubtless refers to the Western Shoshoni. Nothing is said of a similar functionary among the Northern Paiute of Owens Valley. As might be expected from their close association with the Nevada Paviotso, the Northern Paiute of Surprise Valley have the shaman's interpreter. The only other groups for which this office has been noted are the Seed Eater, White Knives, and Salmon Eater bands of Shoshoni in Idaho. The interpreter in these bands is often referred to as the "pipe-lighter," probably as the result of his function of lighting the practitioner's pipe during the ceremony. In an appreciable number of details such as leading the singing, exhorting the shaman to banish the cause of illness, as well as interpreting the shaman's hasty mumbled remarks, the duties of the shaman's speaker among these Shoshoni and the Paviotso are significantly similar.[142] In view of the existence of the shaman's assistant both on the western and the eastern margins of the Basin area, further field work may reveal a wider distribution of the institution in this area.[143]

In the southern part of the Plateau, shamans' assistants appear either in the curing ceremony or in the shamanistic performances. Among the Klamath, Tenino, Takelma, Wishram, and the Sanpoil and Nespelem, the assistant acts as spokesman or interpreter. In addition to the speaker, the shamans of the Sanpoil, Nespelem, and Tenino employ several assistants who aid the shaman in the course of the curing performance. The Klamath interpreter acts both in the shamanistic performance and at the curing.[144]

[142] Steward, *Owens Valley Paiute*, 315; Kelly, *Surprise Valley Paiute*, 193; Hoebel, *Shoshone Religion*, ms.; Harris, *Field notes*, ms.

[143] The appearance of the shaman's speaker among three Shoshoni bands and the Paviotso considerably extends the distribution of this functionary. Spier, *Klamath Ethnography*, 269, indicated the absence in the Basin of this office on the basis of the information then available.

[144] Spier, *Klamath Ethnography*, 113, 124; Sapir, *Religious Ideas of the Takelma Indians*, 43; Spier and Sapir, *Wishram Ethnography*, 246; Ray, *The Sanpoil and Nespelem*, 204; Murdock, *Tenino field notes*, ms.

The shaman's speaker who acts as an interpreter is also reported for northern California. The Achomawi, Atsugewi, Modoc, and Wintu shamans use interpreters in their curing rites. The Sinkyone shaman's helpers lead the singing, but nothing is said about these assistants acting as spokesmen.[145]

With the Northern Maidu, the shaman's assistant has an entirely different rôle, that of clown. When the shaman communes with the spirits, the assistant mocks and apes his actions in order to amuse the spectators. A clown also takes part in the dedication of a new dance house. At this performance, he keeps up a running conversation with the shaman, who is the ceremonial director, repeating that official's words in such a way as to call forth laughter from the spectators. As Spier points out, such clowns appear in the dances of the Kuksu cult; and the Northern Maidu performer seems to be linked with those in the secret society performances.[146] The clowns do not seem to be historically related to the shaman's interpreter, who is known from the present data among only a small number of northern Californian peoples, commonly in the Plateau as far north as the Columbia river, and among several tribes in the Basin. In this area, incomplete information does not permit an accurate statement of the limits for the distribution of the office.

Another assistant sometimes employed by the Paviotso practitioner is the woman dancer who follows the shaman around the fire during the curing rites. Dancing by anyone but the shaman in curing practices is generally quite rare among neighboring tribes. The participation of a female dancer in the shamanistic performances of two Shoshoni bands, the White Knives and the Salmon Eaters, has recently been established. As she follows the shaman in the ritual, the dancer carries a winnowing-tray containing seeds, a practice identical with the Paviotso custom. This assistant among these Shoshoni is asked to serve only when the shaman is treating a female patient or in connection with a curing performance held to drive away an epidemic.[147] I have found no

---

[145] Angulo, *Religious Feeling*, 356–357; Park, *Atsugewi field notes*, ms.; Spier, *Klamath Ethnography*, 268 (summary of information from Meacham for the Modoc); Du Bois, *Wintu Ethnography*, 107–108; Nomland *Sinkyone Notes*, 168.

[146] Dixon, *The Northern Maidu*, 271, 286, 315–318; Spier, *Klamath Ethnography*, 268.

[147] Harris, *Field notes*, ms.

analogue to the Paviotso performer elsewhere in western North America. Material from other Great Basin groups, however, may extend the distribution in this area of the practice, but it seems doubtful that the participation of a woman dancer in the curing rites is known widely in surrounding regions.

REGALIA

Distinctive costumes and other emblems worn by shamans to indicate the possession of supernatural power are found generally in the Plateau and northern California. A head-dress of woodpecker scalps is worn by the Klamath and Shasta shamans, but elsewhere in northern California this is the regalia of such dancers as those who participate in the Yurok and Hupa Jumping Dance. The Northern Maidu Kuksu spirit-impersonators also wear belts of these scalps as well as other feather regalia. Further north, in the Plateau, the shaman's power is advertised by various devices. The shamanistic powers of the Sanpoil and Nespelem are symbolically represented on clothing, the common symbol of a shaman being a red band around the arms or the body of the shirt or dress with still other emblems used to denote special powers. The Southern Okanagon shamans indicate the sources of their powers by lines tattoed on the face or by various distinctive features of costume emblematic of spirits. For each power there is a particular symbol. Still another emblem is used by some of the Thompson shamans, who carry staffs painted with symbolic representations of the guardian spirits.[148] Apparently, however, there is a distinction between the symbolic representation of powers among the several Plateau tribes and the shamanistic regalia of the northern Californian peoples. The feather ornaments and head-dresses of the California shamans are clearly linked with the dance regalia of the northwestern part of the state and that of the Kuksu society. The Plateau power-devices, on the other hand, may be related to the northern Plains practice of representing on shields, dress, or the skin covering of tipis the supernatural experiences and guardian spirits of the individual owners of these objects.

[148] Spier, *Klamath Ethnography*, 110, 271–272; Dixon, *The Shasta*, 481; *The Northern Maidu*, 149, 284; Kroeber, *Handbook*, 56; Goddard, *Life and Culture of the Hupa*, 86; Ray, *The Sanpoil and Nespelem*, 48–49; Cline and others, *The Southern Okanagon*, ms.; Teit, *The Thompson Indians*, 360.

Moreover, the regalia in northern California seems to be used only in performances, whereas in the Plateau emblems of power are generally carried or worn at all times.

Shamanistic regalia is at a minimum among the Paviotso. Some shamans wear special dress when curing; others paint their faces and bodies in designs revealed to them by their powers. Head-dresses or other special emblems of shamanistic office seem to be unknown. This seems to be the case likewise, as far as is known, with other Basin tribes. At least shamanistic regalia has not so far been reported for this area.

Religious regalia is also often absent in California, for ceremonial head-dresses have been noted only for the Achomawi, Atsugewi, and Yokuts, and for those tribes mentioned above. As in northern California, regalia belongs largely to the dancers and performers in the various non-shamanistic rituals performed in this area.[149] It may well be, however, that the interest in the spectacular dances of the northwest, the rituals of the Kuksu society and the non-shamanistic rites of the central and southern region has led investigators to neglect shamanistic regalia. At any rate, negative evidence on this point is usually not available. Therefore, we cannot be entirely certain about the absence of shamans' insignia, emblems and special dress over most of the state.

PARAPHERNALIA

As we have seen, the curing paraphernalia of the Paviotso shaman consists of several feathers, usually from the eagle, a pipe, tobacco, beads, a rattle, red and white paint, and sometimes a bone tube or whistle. All of these objects are stored in a skin bag. The shaman acquires his paraphernalia in obedience to the instructions given him by the spirit from which he derives his power. A particular object, often even the entire kit, has a fetishistic meaning for the shaman. The loss of the eagle-feathers or other parts of the paraphernalia will result in the unfortunate shaman's sickness and loss of power.

The data on the shaman's paraphernalia for many of the neigh-

---

[149] Dixon, *Notes on Achomawi and Atsugewi*, 219; Park, *Atsugewi field notes*, ms.; Kroeber, *Handbook*, 433, 508, 640, 660.

boring tribes are meager. It is therefore impossible to undertake a detailed comparison of all shamanistic equipment, but it will be useful to indicate the distribution of such elements as the rattle, the use of drums in shamanistic performances, and feathers attached to sticks.

Two varieties of rattles have been described for the Paviotso; one, the dangling dew-claw type, is shaken with a jerking motion. The other, shaken similarly, has a drum of stiff dry skin which contains pebbles.

The deer-hooflet rattle is not commonly used by the shamans of neighboring tribes. So far, it has not been reported definitely for any of the Basin tribes to the east of the Paviotso, but rattles of any kind are not noted in the scanty literature on this area. It is said that the shamans in two Shoshoni bands, the Salmon Eaters and White Knives, have canes about four feet long with eagle-feathers and other things such as small deer-hoofs attached to them. That this device is employed as a rattle during the curing performance is not clear. It is recorded, however, that the practitioners of these bands shake a rattle to accompany the singing of their curing rites. The shamans among Northern Paiute of Surprise Valley use a dew-claw rattle similar to the Paviotso instrument, whereas those of the Owens Valley Paiute have the common Californian cocoon-rattle for shamanistic performances.[150] It appears, therefore, as the data now stand, that the use by shamans of the jangling deer-hooflet rattle is confined in the Basin to the Paviotso of Nevada, the closely affiliated band of Northern Paiute in the Surprise Valley of California, and possibly several Shoshoni bands.

In California the rattle of dew-claws is widely used, not in curing but in connection with other rites. As Kroeber has pointed out, in northern California it is associated with girls' adolescence ceremonies. Specifically, the deer-hoof rattle is used in the girls' dance among the Karok, Tolowa, Klamath, Shasta, Achomawi, Atsugewi, Northeastern Maidu, and Wintu. In the southern part of the state, a rattle of this type has been reported for the Luiseño and Diegueño. Among the Luiseño it is used in hunters' rites,

[150] Harris, *Field notes*, ms.; Kelly, *Surprise Valley Paiute*, 191; Steward, *Owens Valley Paiute*, 278, 313.

among the Diegueño in mourning ceremonies.[151] When we come to
the tribes of the lower Colorado and in the Southwest, the deer-
hoof rattle is replaced by the gourd rattle.[152] Clearly this latter
type of instrument is not characteristic of the Great Basin. To
date it has not been reported for a single group.

The shaman's deer-hooflet rattle is not widely known in the
Plateau, but it has been noted for the Wishram, Klallam, Thompson, Lillooet, and Nez Percé. This is distinct from the Klamath
usage noted above, where a rattle of this type appears in connection with the girls' rites. The Nez Percé, Wishram, and Klallam
rattles may be linked with those used in the initiation ceremonies
to the south, for they appear to be similar in style. The Thompson
and Lillooet, on the other hand, fasten bunches of deer-claws to
the feet and knees. These jangling ornaments are customarily
worn in shamanistic performances as well as in non-curative
dances.[153]

The other type of shaman's rattle, the drum of dried skin containing gravel, used by the Paviotso, may be a local adaptation.
I find it noted only for the Owens Valley Paiute. The idea of a
container of pebbles fastened to a stick may have been adapted
from the cocoon-rattles that are widely used in California. This
latter type of instrument is known to some of the Paviotso, but
it is never used by shamans. On the other hand among their Californian neighbors such as the Owens Valley Paiute, Yokuts, Miwok, Pomo, Yuki, Maidu, and Atsugewi, the rattle is commonly
employed by the shamans.[154]

In connection with the suggestion that the skin and pebble
rattle and the cocoon type are related, it may be of interest to
note the terms of the Owens Valley Paiute for both instruments.
The rattle made of skin is known as tsavaiya (the Paviotso designate both this type and the deer-hooflet rattle by the term wisábaya). The cocoon rattle is called tuvoᵛtsávaiya. The first type

[151] Kroeber, *Handbook*, 106, 127, 314, 419, 665, 723, 823, 862; Spier, *Klamath Ethnography*, 89, 323; Dixon, *The Shasta*, 458; *The Northern Maidu*, 236; Park, *Atsugewi field
notes*, ms.; Du Bois, *Wintu Ethnography*, 52, 124.

[152] The distribution of gourd rattles is given by Spier, *Havasupai Ethnography*, 289–290.

[153] Spier and Sapir, *Wishram Ethnography*, 201; Gunther, *Klallam Ethnography*, 298;
Teit, *The Thompson Indians*, 364, 384; *The Lillooet*, 287; Spinden, *The Nez Percé*, 230.

[154] Steward, *Owens Valley Paiute*, 278; Kroeber, *Handbook*, 420, 823; Park *Atsugewi*,
field notes, ms.

is used only at feasts in the sweat-house after rabbit-drives. The latter type appears both on these occasions and also in shamanistic curing.[155]

The drum has no place in the Paviotso shamanistic complex. In fact, drums were entirely unknown until about 1885, when they were introduced by the Bannock in connection with a "war dance." Even then the instrument did not become firmly fixed in Paviotso culture, for it seems to have fallen into disuse after a time, to be reintroduced by the Bannock some thirty-five years later.

Drums do not figure prominently in the literature on the Great Basin. Lowie mentions two types for the Lemhi Shoshoni, a hand-drum and a large drum. There is no suggestion that either is used by shamans.[156] This seems to be the only reference to these instruments. The absence, or failure to report the use of such a device, also holds for California, where, with the exception of the foot-drum in the area of the Kuksu cult, drums are unknown or are of little importance.[157]

Turning to the Plateau, we find again that drums are not as a rule used by the shamans. It seems quite likely that, as Spier points out, the southern Plateau was probably, until very recently, a drumless area. Among the Klamath, for example, the hand-drum was in use before the whites came, but it has no great antiquity. It is used only in social dances. The hand-drum, sometimes called the tambourine, has been noted in the Plateau for the Thompson, Shuswap, Northern Okanagon, Nez Percé, and Wishram; Spier adds the Kutenai, Coeur d'Alêne, Wasco, and Warm Springs, but there is no evidence that it is ever used by shamans of any of these tribes.[158]

The use of drums, not the hand-drum, however, is recorded for the Wishram and Klallam. The usual form of the Wishram drum is a plank laid before a row of drummers who beat on it with

---

[155] Steward, *Owens Valley Paiute*, 278.

[156] Lowie, *The Northern Shoshone*, 206.

[157] Kroeber, *Handbook*, 824.

[158] Spier, *Prophet Dance*, 45–46; *Klamath Ethnography*, 89; Teit, *The Thompson Indians*, 383–384; *The Shuswap*, 575, 787; Cline and others, *The Southern Okanagon*, ms. (information on the Northern Okanagon); Spinden, *The Nez Percé*, 230; Spier and Sapir, *Wishram Ethnography*, 201.

pieces of wood. This instrument is commonly used in a shaman's curing practice and in the hand-game. In one instance of curing among the Klallam, it is recorded that people had drums and sticks to help the shaman by beating time. That these were of the type described is not altogether clear. The Tenino of Warm Springs likewise employ in their curing rites beaters who pound with sticks on a long pole laid on the floor.[159]

Clearly, in view of this survey, the association of the hand-drum and shamanistic practices noted for several regions of the world is not characteristic of the Plateau, Great Basin, and California. In fact, drumming in any fashion does not figure prominently in the shamanistic rites of western North America.

Feathers, usually the tail-feathers and down of eagles, form an extremely important part of the Paviotso shaman's parapher- nalia, partly because of the common belief that they are symbolic of the shaman's power. These feathers, moreover, are used by all shamans in the curing performance, especially in connection with the stick which is planted near the patient's head during the rites.

The use of eagle-feathers in curing and other shamanistic per- formances is widespread. In fact it seems almost universal among the tribes of western North America. But the particular way in which the Paviotso shamans utilize feathers has not been generally noted in the practices of neighboring areas. The scanty data on Great Basin usages do not permit a definite statement for that region. Several scattered instances of the use of feathers in cura- tive rites suggest that the practice may be more general among these tribes. One shaman among the Owens Valley Paiute is re- ported to have stuck long sticks bearing eagle-feathers into the ground around his patients, but this was not apparently done generally by shamans. Shamans among the White Knives and Salmon Eater bands of Shoshoni commonly use eagle-feathers in their curing ceremonies. Feathers are attached to a cane which is placed in the ground by the patient's head. This practice is clearly similar in details to the Paviotso custom.[160]

A somewhat different practice is reported for the Northeastern

---

[159] Spier and Sapir, *Wishram Ethnography*, 201; Gunther, *Klallam Ethnography*, 302; Murdock, *Tenino field notes*, ms.

[160] Steward, *Owens Valley Paiute*, 316; Harris, *Field notes*, ms.

Maidu, who plant feather wands on the graves of chiefs and shamans. The same type of wand is also used in a performance for the
novice shaman. These wands are set upon the roof of the house
in which the ceremony is held, and during the performance the
shamans offer them to the spirits. The wand figured by Dixon is
strikingly similar to those used by the Paviotso shamans in curing.[161] Possibly these Northern Maidu wands, employed in a different context, are historically related to the Paviotso and Shoshoni feather-sticks.

The Ghost Dance of the Kaibab is reported to have involved
the planting of a feather wand. In this performance, a cedar pole
about two feet high was planted in the center of the circle. Two
feathers, one a tail-feather painted red, the other a soft white
feather taken from under the tail of an eagle, were suspended by
a string from the top of the pole. Sometimes, instead of the pole,
the prophet put up a stick of service-berry wood which had been
nicely smoothed; from it the same two feathers hung. The Chemehuevi shamans formerly used "a simple cat's-claw staff hooked
at the end" in the curing performance, but nothing is said of the
use of feathers in this connection.[162]

The Havasupai prayer-sticks planted at the springs are similar
in several details to the feather wands of both the Northern Maidu
and the Paviotso. They differ largely in having a shorter stick
and in being made of the feathers of turkey and pinon bird as well
as of the eagle. There is no association, however, between prayer-
plumes and shamanistic rites among the Havasupai. As Spier
points out, the Havasupai usage represents an elaborate Pueblo
practice in an attenuated form.[163] It may well be, however, that
the feather wands of the Northeastern Maidu, Paviotso, the two
Shoshoni bands, and Kaibab link eventually with the prayer-
sticks of the Southwest.

CAUSE OF DISEASE

Shamanistic curing is closely linked with the conception that
sickness results from supernatural agencies. In western North

---

[161] Dixon, *The Northern Maidu*, 243–244; 275.

[162] Sapir, *Kaibab field notes*, ms.; Kelly, *Chemehuevi Shamanism*, 132.

[163] Spier, *Havasupai Ethnography*, 286, 290.

America several of these beliefs play important rôles in the shamanistic complex of the several tribes. In addition to the belief that illness is a manifestation of spiritual forces, certain ailments and injuries are here regarded—as is often the case elsewhere in the world—as linked with natural causes and accidents. These are usually treated with herbs, roots, and other simple "home remedies." Such curative practices may involve the possession of supernatural power or they may be entirely in the hands of laymen. We shall consider here those diseases that are attributed to supernatural causes and consequently involve shamanistic practices in their treatment. It must be remembered, however, that the distinction is not always clear-cut; the Paviotso shaman not only sucks out disease-objects and returns lost souls, but he also treats by suction wounds caused by bullets and arrows.

Concepts of disease are on the whole fairly similar throughout the region west of the Rocky Mountains. Thus, the Paviotso are at one with most of the neighboring tribes in the belief that sickness results from the practice of sorcery, from intrusive objects, soul loss, and from the appearance of ghosts. To be sure, these concepts are not all distinct but may be combined with a variety of interpretations. The belief that illness results from the loss of the soul may be associated with the idea that ghosts try to steal away the souls of the living, as in the case of the Paviotso. Although, then, the several disease-concepts are widespread in western North America, their distributions do not coincide. One example will serve to illustrate. The conception that sickness results from soul loss is prominent with the Paviotso and among many northern Californian and southern Plateau tribes, but it is entirely lacking among the Klamath.[164] Moreover, these several concepts are often somewhat differently combined and interpreted among the several tribes. Still, beliefs that ailments are the result of soul loss, the appearance of ghosts, intrusive objects, and the practice of witchcraft, are so nearly universal in this region as to suggest that the Plateau, Great Basin, and California areas are a unit in respect at least to these generalized conceptions.

Recognized differences in the New World distributions of several disease-concepts are to some ethnologists evidence that cer-

[164] Spier, *Klamath Ethnography*, 122.

tain of these beliefs were introduced earlier than others. Thus Lowie has suggested that the presence in western North America of the belief in soul loss as a cause of disease is due to a relatively late borrowing from Siberia. It may well be, as he argues, that the basic disease-concept of the New World is that of intrusion, but certainly among many western tribes it is coupled with the belief in soul loss. In fact, on the basis of present data for this region, soul loss is found among an appreciably greater number of tribes than there are groups in which the notion is unknown. Evidence from the rest of the continent suggests that soul loss is largely confined to the far west, with intrusion as the dominant disease-concept elsewhere. This alone, however, does not prove the relative recency of the introduction of an Asiatic element into western North America. It may be regarded only as one of the possible explanations of the more limited distribution of the idea that the loss of the soul causes sickness. Without corroboratory evidence for such an assumption, it would be nearly as plausible, if not equally so, to argue that the concept is as old, or at least almost as old, in the New World as disease-object intrusion. The latter suggestion is indeed strengthened on distributional grounds by citing the case mentioned by Lowie, of the Fuegeians' belief in disease resulting from spontaneous wanderings of souls, and the sporadic appearance of similar ideas among other South Americans that have been tabulated by Clements.[165] That this type of distributional evidence at once raises questions of paramount interest to the reconstruction of culture history is widely recognized. And this is only one among many examples of the difficulties, also the dangers, inherent in attempts to reconstruct time-sequences merely on the basis of distributional evidence which moreover, is often crucially incomplete.

As these disease-concepts have been analyzed and their distributions over the world have been mapped and tabulated by Clements,[166] it will not be necessary to re-examine the data in full here. The purposes of this study will best be served by limiting the discussion to the evidence for the suggestion made above, namely, that the Paviotso share with the neighboring tribes the generalized

---

[165] Lowie, *Primitive Religion*, 176–180; Clements, *Primitive Concepts of Disease*, 196–197.
[166] Clements, *Primitive Concepts of Disease*.

concepts of disease mentioned, at the same time recognizing distinct local differences of interpretation as well as the several instances in which distributions do not coincide.

The Paviotso belief that sickness results from dreams is by no means universal among western tribes. According to Paviotso thinking, these dreams are involuntary and are in themselves the cause, not an omen, of illness. Further, it is not necessarily one's own dream that results in sickness. For instance, the dreams of parents or other relatives may cause the sickness of a child. This conception of dreaming as a cause of disease, especially the involuntary nature of the dreams, is strongly emphasized in Paviotso belief. The constantly recurring fear of dreams and the almost daily repeating of prayers that help counteract their evil effects indicate something of the intense preoccupation with this potential source of grief.

The belief that dreams are an extremely potent source of illness has been reported for several Basin groups, the Seed Eater, Salmon Eater, and White Knives bands of Shoshoni in Idaho and Nevada, and the Northern Ute. The conceptions of these people are significantly similar to the Paviotso notion; dreams are directly causative and involuntary and may bring sickness either to the dreamer or to a relative. Thus, when a man dies for no apparent reason his relatives frequently blame the widow's dreams for causing the fatal illness.[167] More intensive field investigations may reveal that this belief is held by still other Basin tribes.

Over most of California and generally in the Plateau, dreams that are linked with sickness are prophetic, not directly the cause of the illness. Here the characteristic belief is that the appearance of death or sickness in dream-experiences foreshadows the actual event but is not necessarily the cause. This is clearly distinct from the strong emphasis in the Basin on dreams as the causative agent.

The dream-basis of both sickness and success in life is most highly elaborated on the lower Colorado river and among the neighboring Maricopa. As with the Paviotso, dreams here are not prophetic but are directly responsible for illness. This concept is

[167] Hoebel, *Shoshone Religion*, ms.; Harris, *Field notes*, ms.; Cooke, *Northern Ute field notes*, ms.

best described for the Maricopa, who believe that contact with certain things in dream-experiences brings on sickness. Thus illness is not due to the activities of spirits, but results directly from the dream. The Mohave and Yuma also have the idea that dreams cause sickness, that the soul of the dreamer is affected by his experiences in dream-life.[168] This belief is not held by all the Yumans, however, for the Havasupai believe that spirits are the cause of illness and the Walapai hold that sickness is due to the activity of spirits. It is said that among the latter people dreams "bring or foretell good or bad luck," but it is not clear that they are directly causative.[169] The limits of the distribution of the concept of dreams as a direct cause of disease cannot be precisely determined from the data that are available at present. There is strong suggestion, however, in the material presented here of an affiliation between the Basin (at least Paviotso, Shoshoni, and Ute) and some of the Yuman tribes.

Antelope Charming

The procedure of shamans who charm antelope for a communal drive has been given in the descriptive account of Paviotso shamanism. The performance of the antelope shaman is the chief non-curing function of shamans. It is noteworthy that the communal drives for ducks, mudhens, and rabbits, important as they are in food-gathering activities, involve no shamanistic activities whatsoever. The ceremonies accompanying the antelope-drive seem on the whole about as elaborate as the curing rites. Moreover, the practices of the antelope shaman give the impression of having a well-established place in the shamanistic pattern. Finally there is no internal evidence to indicate that antelope-charming is more recent in Paviotso culture than other shamanistic rites. It will be of value to survey briefly neighboring tribes for analogous practices.

The closely-related Northern Paiute of Surprise Valley have antelope-charmers who use their power at communal drives. The details of charming here are almost precisely the same as among

[168] Spier, *Yuman Tribes*, 280; Kroeber, *Handbook*, 775; Forde, *Ethnography of the Yuma*, 187 f.

[169] Spier, *Havasupai Ethnography*, 277; Kroeber, ed., *Walapai Ethnography*, 186, 231.

the Paviotso. The Northern Paiute of Owens Valley, however, have no shamanistic activities in connection with the communal game-drives.[170] Communal drives have been noted among still other Basin tribes, often with no evidence that shamanistic practices are connected with securing game in this fashion. The Gosiute of Utah drive antelope into a V-shaped runway constructed of logs and brush, and hunters hidden at the apex of the chute kill the animals. There is no indication that the shaman plays any particular rôle in this activity, nor is there mention that supernatural power is invoked in order to insure success in finding game. Deer, antelope and buffalo are surrounded by men on horseback or on foot and killed by the Lemhi Shoshoni and the Northern Ute, but no shamanistic performances are recorded in connection with these activities.[171]

Antelope-charming has recently been noted for one of the eastern neighbors of the Paviotso, the White Knives, and also for another Shoshoni band, the Salmon Eaters. The presence of shamanistic rites in connection with a communal antelope-drive appears to be somewhat more characteristic of the White Knives than of the band to the east. Antelope-charming in these groups is similar in a substantial number of details to Paviotso practices. Specifically, resemblances are found in such details as the construction of the corral under the leadership of the antelope shaman, the scraping of a bow string wrapped around a folded or rolled antelope-hide, singing to charm the animals, the first antelope killed given to the shaman, tabu against the presence of menstruating and pregnant women. Certain features found in these Shoshoni drives but unknown to the Paviotso include blood spurting from the mouth and nose of the shaman to indicate control over the animals, special attention paid to the leader of the herd, horns worn in the ceremony by at least some shamans. Bleeding at the nose and mouth is reminiscent of similar violent reactions experienced by many novices in the Plateau when in the course of the quest power is conferred. Unlike the Paviotso antelope shamans, the charmers among these Shoshoni do not

[170] Kelly, *Surprise Valley Paiute*, 83–86; Steward, *Owens Valley Paiute*, 253.
[171] Chamberlin, *Ethno-Botany of the Gosiute*, 335–336; Lowie, *The Northern Shoshone*, 185; *Shoshonean Ethnography*, 199.

appear to possess curing power; they are, however, regarded as shamans.[172] Without disregarding the important differences between Shoshoni and Paviotso practice and belief, we perceive that significant similarities appear. No other accounts of antelope-charming among the people of this area have so far come to light. In view, however, of the scanty material on the Basin tribes, this cannot be taken as very strong evidence that these practices are not to be found among other groups in this area.

It may be of interest to note that the antelope shamans of Nevada and Surprise Valley frequently use a rasp in their performances in place of the deer-hooflet and the skin-and-pebble rattle used in curing rites. The notched-stick rasp appears among the Paviotso in the charming rite, but more often a string wound around a stick or a bundle of skins, sometimes a string around a stuffed skin, is scraped. The latter type is the characteristic Surprise Valley instrument. The stick, bone, or horn used to scrape the string may be notched, or, as with the two Shoshoni bands mentioned above, it may be smooth. The latter form of the rasp does not seem to be widely known. The notched-stick rasp, however, is used commonly throughout the Basin, in the Plateau area, the Plains, and the Southwest. In California, it has been reported only for the Salinans.[173] In this trait, then, California-Basin affiliations are clearly absent.

The musical bow, mentioned in two Paviotso accounts of antelope-charming, suggests a linkage with California, possibly through the Mono Lake Paiute. This instrument has not so far been reported for any of the eastern neighbors of the Paviotso. Its presence in Owens Valley seems doubtful, but Steward describes a musical bow for the closely-related Paiute of Mono Lake. In addition, he mentions a Field Museum specimen from the Western Mono. Elsewhere in California, this instrument has been noted for the Pomo, Maidu, Yokuts, and Diegueño, and according to Kroeber it was probably still more widely known. The Californians played the instrument for pleasure and in some instances for communicating with spirits.[174] The Paviotso practice of employing

[172] Harris, *Field notes*, ms.

[173] Lowie, *Northern Shoshone*, 219; Spier, *Klamath Ethnography*, 229; Kroeber, *Handbook*, 824.

[174] Steward, *Owens Valley Paiute*, 278; Kroeber, *Handbook*, 824.

the musical bow only in shamanistic rites connected with antelope-charming may have a basis in the last-mentioned usage of the people to the west. The association of the instrument with ritual hunting is, however, unique to the Paviotso.

Shamanistic charming of game for communal drives is not a common procedure either in the Plateau area or in California. The drive is specifically lacking among the Klamath and Wishram, and among the Sanpoil and Nespelem it is accompanied by very simple magical rites which are not connected with shamanistic practices.[175] Generally, praying and magical practices are thought necessary for success in hunting as well as in other ventures, but the particular cluster of practices found in Paviotso antelope-charming certainly has no analogues either in specific detail or in the larger aggregate of customs anywhere in the Plateau.

Californians come together for communal drives of deer and antelope, but these drives are usually of the surround type, in contrast to the corral with flaring wings. Shamanistic charming of the animals does not seem to be practised, although magical rites are performed. From the information at hand, the Paviotso practices of charming do not apparently link with any of the rites found in California.

Turning to the Yuman tribes on the western fringe of the Southwest area, we find that communal drives in which deer, antelope, and mountain sheep are captured appear to have a well-recognized place in the activities of these people. At least the Havasupai and Walapai are reported to drive large game to positions where concealed hunters can shoot them easily. Magic and charms insure success for these undertakings, but shamanistic practices in connection with these hunts have not been noted. Apparently the Maricopa do not drive game, but an ambush for which several men have performed a preliminary ritual thought to insure success, is employed in deer-hunting. Shamanistic ceremonies do not appear, however, in connection with these pursuits.[176]

---

[175] Spier, *Klamath Ethnography*, 158; Spier and Sapir, *Wishram Ethnography*, 180; Ray, *The Sanpoil and Nespelem*, 77 f.

[176] Spier, *Havasupai Ethnography*, 110; *Yuman Tribes*, 69; Kroeber, ed., *Walapai Ethnography*, 61, 65, 68.

Further evidence that magical charming of game in the Southwest is genetically distinct from the Paviotso practices is to be found in Beaglehole's recently published study of hunting rituals of the Hopi. This point is borne out by the descriptive material on Hopi hunting practices and the attendant rituals as well as by his comparative notes on the Southwest.[177] Clearly the rites and beliefs of the Hopi in connection with hunting are distinctly different from the shamanistic practices of the Paviotso antelope-drive. An exception to the general absence in the Southwest of shamanistic direction of communal drives along Paviotso lines occurs among the Navaho. Hill has recently recorded accounts of Navaho practices which are strikingly analogous to Paviotso shamanistic antelope-charming. Features of the Navaho antelope ceremony which suggest this similarity are: direction of the hunt by a shaman, ceremonial selection of the site of the camp, corral marked off with ceremony by the leader, the use of scouts or runners in the hunt, corresponding rites for charming the antelope preceding the actual drive and after the construction of the corral, and ritual disposal of parts of the game.[178]

In still another part of western North America, communal drives of game are associated with shamanistic beliefs and practices. Among the Plains tribes, buffalo were commonly driven through flaring wings into the corral, where they were killed. Shamanistic charming in connection with these drives has been briefly reported for several Plains tribes, for instance the Crow, Assiniboin, and Arapaho. Calling buffalo or deer among the Crow constituted a particular form of shamanistic activity based on a specific vision. The animal-charmer practised either in connection with the two customary methods of driving game or at a time when food was badly needed. The performance held the night before the drive included singing, imitation of the buffalo or deer, the sending out of scouts, and the use of buffalo-skulls. The shamanistic charming of buffalo and elk among the Arapaho and Assiniboin seem, from the incomplete descriptions available, to be quite similar to the practices followed by the Crow.[179]

[177] Beaglehole, *Hopi Hunting and Hunting Ritual*.
[178] Hill, *Navaho Field notes*, ms.
[179] Lowie, *Religion of the Crow Indians*, 354–359; Denig, *Indian Tribes of the Upper Missouri*, 532–533, 537; Kroeber, *The Arapaho*, 22–23, 436–437.

In spite of the differences between the charming rites of the western Plains and the Paviotso, significant similarities are to be noted. Association of ceremonial charming with a particular type of drive noted, use of a corral, supernatural calling of animals as a function of the shaman, a specific kind of power required for the rite, singing and imitating animals in order to charm them, are all features that point to a connection between Plains and Paviotso practices. To be sure, there are important gaps in the distribution of these rites, particularly in the Great Basin, but these do not as yet provide conclusive negative evidence. We have a definite suggestion in the field material collected by Harris among the White Knives and Salmon Eater bands of Shoshoni that antelope-charming involving a substantial number of practices similar to Paviotso usages may have a wider distribution in the Basin than has been heretofore suspected. Further work among other tribes of this area may provide materials that will more accurately show the linkages with the Plains.

SUMMARY

It has been possible here to trace the distributions in western North America of certain shamanistic practices and beliefs. Because of the paucity of detailed data, it is impossible at the present time to indicate the spatial limits of all the elements that enter into the complex in this region. Despite the important gaps in our knowledge, suggestive indications of relationships emerge from the survey.

It is evident that Paviotso shamanism has a general basis common to the practices found in the Plateau, Great Basin, and parts of California. Supernatural power bestowed by animal and natural spirits, relatively simple rituals, shaman's function largely that of curing, shamanistic power used either for curing or for causing sickness, and the social prominence of the shaman are generalized aspects of shamanism that hold for most of the tribes of these areas, and some of these features are, of course, even more widely known. Beyond this common basis for the shamanistic complex, there is a substantial number of elements in Paviotso practice which have definitely limited distributions among the neighboring peoples. Some of these practices indicate cultural affiliations with one or several of the surrounding areas; still others may be the result of local development.

It emerges also from this survey that certain features, such as shamanistic winter performances and the novice dance in the Plateau, are not known to the Paviotso. On the other hand, some beliefs that form a part of the local complex are much more strongly emphasized elsewhere in North America. The importance attached in the Plateau to the power quest is in sharp contrast with the relatively insignificant rôle which this practice plays in Paviotso shamanism. Thus, although the Paviotso have much in common with the Plateau, several of the elements that give to the Plateau complex its characteristic content and form are locally unknown. In fact, the affiliations between the Paviotso and the Plateau appear largely in the generalized basis of belief in sources of power, curing practices, clairvoyance, and witchcraft. This statement is further significant when it is recalled that these similarities are particularly evident in those elements that are also widely known beyond the limits of these areas.

Unquestionably Paviotso—probably all Basin—shamanism is less elaborate than the Plateau complex in content. This simplicity is marked by the absence in the Basin of those ceremonies just mentioned—an extended power-quest, winter performances, and the novice dance. These are by no means, however, confined to the Plateau, for the quest is known widely in the New World and the novice dance appears in California as far south as the Northern Maidu.

The distributions of certain other Paviotso practices and beliefs yield evidence of significant linkages in other directions. Ghosts of the dead and water-babies or dwarfs are a source of power in northern California, among the Paviotso, several Shoshoni bands, and in the Plains. In this feature, then, Paviotso belief links both with the west in northern California and with the east with several Basin peoples and the western Plains. Northward in the Plateau, spirits of animals and natural phenomena predominate, and in the Basin animal and natural spirits share attention with ghosts and dwarfs.

The simple quest found in the Basin also occurs in the western Southwest among at least the Maricopa and Walapai. The simplicity of the deliberate search for power is not alone evidence of affiliations between the two areas, but the similarity of the experience involved in seeking and acquiring power in this fashion suggests possibilities of linkages. Moreover, this taken in connection with an appreciable number of other similarities both in elements such as dreams as a source of illness, perhaps the use of feather wands, and other like elements, as well as important resemblances in interpretation, adds weight to the evidence that suggestive interrelationships between these areas exist.

Involuntary dreams in which power is bestowed on the dreamer appear sporadically in the Plateau: among the Thompson, Southern Okanagon in connection with inheritance, and among the Klamath combined with the quest experience. Among the Paviotso, as well as a number of other Basin tribes, these experiences are basic to all shamanistic power. Dreams as a source of power appear in parts of northern California, commonly in the rest of the state and in the western Southwest. On the lower Colorado and among some of the other Yumans to the east, dreams receive special emphasis, coloring not only shamanism but all beliefs and activities. In this region, dreams are regarded as an important cause of illness; this strongly suggests an affiliation with the Paviotso, Northern Ute, and Shoshoni beliefs. In fact, the presence of and strong emphasis on this belief in part of the Basin at any rate suggests important connections with the unique dreamlife of the lower Coloradoans.

In the Plateau and California, disease results from witchcraft, intrusive objects, and soul loss. These are likewise known to the Paviotso along with the notion that sickness results from involuntary dreams. The Paviotso conception that after a shaman once kills by sorcery he continues without volition, that he is even compelled to continue practising witchcraft, appears to be an unique and specialized belief, perhaps derived from or otherwise related to the idea that involuntary dreams also cause illness.

The shaman's interpreter is common to Plateau, parts of northern California, and several Basin groups, at least Paviotso and Shoshoni. With the Maidu and westward in the area of the Kuksu cult, the assistant becomes a clown and seems to have no historical relation to the shaman's talker. If, as Spier suggests, the shaman's interpreter, as the institution appears in the southern Plateau, northern California and part of the Basin, links with the chief's speaker widely known in western America,[180] there is a suggestion of older connections which have been subject to important modifications in several localized areas.

The performances of the Paviotso antelope shaman are clearly not related to any of the magical rites employed in securing game in the Plateau, California and, with the exception of the Navaho, the Southwest. On the other hand, shamanistic charming of game unquestionably affiliates with the western Plains practices of calling buffalo at communal drives.

Little has been said of the elements that are probably the result of local growth. In the absence of more detailed material from neighboring tribes, it would be useless and even misleading to assign to local development all the elements not recorded in the literature. It may well be that the woman dancer in the curing performance, and numerous other minor parts of the complex are the result of indigenous growth, but the determination of these points depends upon convincing negative evidence from neighboring tribes. That such elements have not been noted in the fragmentary accounts of Basin cultures does not constitute valid evidence that they are not to be found in the practices of this region.

It is clear, then, that in the setting of western North American cultures, Paviotso shamanism is largely built on generalized beliefs and practices. The number of elements involved in the complex is relatively small, with the rituals meager and simple. Nevertheless, some important features are doubtless peculiarly local in growth, and others are shared only with several neighboring tribes. The differing distributions of distinct parts of the complex not only establish that Paviotso practices and beliefs are an amalgam of historically diverse elements but in addition yield evidence of the multiplicity of cultural affiliations which have contributed to its growth.

[180] Spier, *Klamath Ethnography*, 269.

IV. Conclusions

The distributional data presented in the last chapter reveal a significant number of affiliations of the Paviotso shamanistic complex with the practices of certain neighboring tribes. These indicated interrelationships have an important bearing on problems connected with the reconstruction of the culture history of this region. It therefore remains for us to consider the broader implications in the evidence of these spatial connections, as well as the limitations of such data for inferring the history of growth in aboriginal American cultures.

Foremost among the conclusions suggested by the geographical distributions of elements in Paviotso shamanistic practices is that important linkages with surrounding cultures are clearly indicated. In some practices there is evidence of affiliation with the Plateau; others point to connections with California, the western Plains, or the non-pueblo Southwest. On the other hand, a substantial number of similarities in attitude, in phrasing, as well as resemblances in several unique elements, link Paviotso shamanism to the practices found among the several Great Basin tribes for which reporting has been at all adequate. If the Paviotso position can be regarded as reasonably typical for the Basin at large, it is clear that the shamanism of this area does not intimately bind these cultures to any one of the surrounding areas. This suggests that it may be in order to reconsider several current views of Basin connections with adjacent areas.

It has long been customary in ethnological literature to treat the Basin as part of either the Plateau or the central California area. Accordingly the designation "Plateau Shoshoneans" continues to be used in referring to Basin peoples, with a close connection of the cultures of the two regions expressed or implied. Yet nearly twenty years ago and in several statements since Kroeber has suggested that the two areas have little in common.[1] Unfortunately, neglect of Basin ethnology has blocked the testing of this view by empirical data. The present survey of the distri-

[1] Kroeber, *California Culture Provinces*, 168–169; *Handbook*, 917; *Native Cultures of the Southwest*, 390.

butions of shamanistic practices makes it evident that in this phase of culture the Plateau and the Great Basin have few specific and unique customs in common. The shaman's speaker is perhaps the only distinctive feature shared by several tribes in the two regions, and this trait spills over into northeastern California. Other similarities between the two areas are largely in generalized widely occurring elements, such as animal spirits a source of supernatural power, high social status of the shaman, disease the result of an intrusive pathogenic agent or soul loss, and several practices connected with the curing rite. On the other hand, those features that actually characterize the Plateau shamanistic complex, among others a distinctive and elaborated power quest, usually at puberty, the winter ceremony at which control of spirits is demonstrated by the novice or reaffirmed by the veteran shaman, are unknown among the Paviotso and appear to be absent from the entire Basin. Thus it is clearly apparent that despite certain similarities, Plateau practices are not closely related to those in the Basin.

This conclusion does not imply, however, that important interrelationships between the two areas are not indicated by the distributional evidence. The shaman's assistant among Basin and Plateau peoples already has been mentioned as clearly pointing to a connection. The simple power quest of the Basin may likewise link with practices to the north, although a suggestively similar deliberate seeking of power appears in parts of central California and among the western non-pueblo tribes of the Southwest. It may further be noted in this connection that Spier has made a strong case for a connection between the Ghost Dance movements and the earlier revivalistic cults of the tribes in the northwestern interior Plateau. The complex, embracing the notion of world destruction and renewal with the return of the dead hastened by dances, appears among all the interior tribes from the Babine and Sekani in the north southward to the Paviotso. The evidence presented by Spier indicates that the complex which he designates as the Prophet Dance first developed in the north and penetrated the Basin prior to 1870, where it fostered the several Ghost Dance movements in that area.[2] That this Plateau

[2] Spier, *The Prophet Dance*, 4-24.

influence on the Basin may have been accompanied by an introduction of shamanistic practices and beliefs is not to be disregarded, but the distributional data presented here yield no positive evidence of such importations.

The recognition of central California-Basin affinities has led to
a classification in which these regions are regarded as a single
culture area. Kroeber has been the leading exponent of the contention that a close genetic relationship exists between the Basin
and central California cultures. According to this widely accepted
view, the latter area has been regarded as a cultural hearth, with
the Basin as an adjunct displaying only a simple version of the
civilization that characterizes the center of development. Thus,
"The Kuksu cult and the institutions associated with it have not
flowed directly into Utah and Idaho, nor even in any measure
into Nevada, but they indicate a dominance of cultural effective-
ness, which, merely in a somewhat lower degree, relates central
California to the Great Basin substantially as the North Pacific
coast is related to the northern Plateau."[3] A comparison of the
shamanistic practices in the two areas does not entirely support
this statement. It has been shown that several elements and
clusters of traits, outstanding in the complex of the Paviotso and
several of their Basin neighbors, such as the concept of dreams
as an immediate cause of illness, unique practices connected with
sorcery, shamanistic charming of game, and some of the paraphernalia, do not appear at all among the tribes to the west. In
numbers these differences are not imposing, but when the influence of certain of these features in the Basin complex on the
dominant attitudes that color much of the culture is taken into
account, a significant distinction is clearly evident. This important
difference is especially apparent when the Paviotso beliefs and
practices connected with sorcery and the dream source of illness
are considered. These are not merely elements that are to be compared to traits elsewhere, for they are deeply rooted in the culture
and are reflected in the crucial attitudes and interests of laymen
and shamans alike. It must be recognized that such weighting and
phrasing are as much the result of historical growth—and their
occurrence, therefore, as important evidence of connection be-

[3] Kroeber, *California Culture Provinces*, 169; *Handbook*, 917.

tween cultures—as those descriptively isolated fragments of cultures so commonly used in their distributional setting to reconstruct relationships. When these factors are taken into consideration, Paviotso shamanistic practices appear in somewhat different perspective. Unquestionably, numerous traits are shared with California; but, as with the resemblances to Plateau elements, the similarities are preponderantly in those generalized basic beliefs and customs which occur widely in the New World. At the same time, the religious practices sufficiently unique to contribute to a characterization of a central California area are significantly lacking among the Paviotso and other Basin people. Equally important in distinguishing the two areas is the conclusion to be drawn from the distributional data that important Paviotso-Shoshoni beliefs and phrasings in shamanism have not appeared west of the Sierra Nevadas.

Added weight to the differences between the two areas is to be found in the distributions of other cultural elements. The folklore is perhaps better known today than any other phase of Great Basin culture. It is, therefore, noteworthy that Gayton's recent analysis of folk-tales in California and the surrounding areas indicates that despite important Basin-California connections, a substantial number of elements in the mythology of California do not appear in the Basin. The map depicting interareal linkages may, from the point of view of the Basin, be said to indicate that a number of Basin tales have penetrated eastern California but have not reached the Yokuts, Miwok, Patwin and other tribes that are usually regarded as forming the nucleus of the central Californian area.[4]

The view formulated by Wissler in his classification of North American cultures into ten areal types involved a somewhat different treatment of Basin cultures. Originally on the basis of the material aspects of life, and later employing the scanty data from this region on religion and social organization, he assigned the Mono-Paviotso groups in the west to the California area, but regarded the cultures of eastern Basin tribes as basically Plains in type.[5] As the incomplete information for the entire Basin stands

[4] Gayton, *Areal Affiliations of California Folktales*, 595–597, Fig. 1, 596.
[5] Wissler, *Material Cultures of North American Indians*, 80–82; *The American Indian*, 222–225.

today, this division seems hardly justified. It is impossible to define as yet the position of Basin material culture in relation to surrounding areas, but it is quite clear that several Shoshoni bands, such as Seed Eater, Salmon Eater, White Knives, possibly Lemhi and other eastern groups, possess shamanistic practices and beliefs substantially similar to those of the Paviotso. This does not, of course, exclude recognition of linkages with the Plains. It is clear that shamanistic charming of game for a communal drive, ghosts and dwarfs a source of power, are at least some of the specific traits that connect Paviotso-Shoshoni with the western Plains. Further indication of connections with this area must await more detailed ethnographic studies in the eastern Basin, among the Shoshoni and the numerous Ute groups.

It now begins to be evident that the relationship of the Great Basin to surrounding areas possibly calls for a formulation somewhat different from those customary in North American ethnology. This does not argue, however, that the Basin can, as far as our knowledge at present goes, be accorded the status of an independent culture area. It would be palpably unjustified to determine the position of these cultures from the distributions of shamanistic practices alone. Moreover, at the present time, evidence is inconclusive that the description of Paviotso practices and beliefs can be taken as reasonably typical for the entire area. But as information comes in, the feeling grows that a substantial number of practices are common to at least a block of Basin tribes.

Whatever cultural autonomy the Basin area may eventually merit, it remains to account for the numerous similarities with the Plateau, California, and possibly western Plains, that appear, as we have seen, largely in generalized, widely-occurring practices. In pointing out a number of important resemblances between central California and Basin cultures, Lowie has suggested that " . . . both these groups, together with other Far Western tribes, may perhaps be conveniently united as representing a single basic ultramontane culture area or stratum marked off from the remainder of the continent."[6] This view is supported by the data of the distributions of several customs and institutions. It must

[6] Lowie, *Cultural Connections of California and Plateau Shoshonean Tribes*, 156.

be recognized, however, that many generalized elements of shamanistic practice suggest relations with a much wider area. Moreover, local developments have unquestionably brought into existence unique practices and phrasings which clearly differentiate the shamanism of the several areas in western North America. Perhaps the accumulating detailed ethnographic materials will inspire further distributional studies of non-material traits, and these may reveal additional evidence of local developments. Only then will we be in a position to make definitive areal characterizations. Indeed, this situation is foreshadowed by Spier's demonstration that there are at least four types of girls' adolescence rites in the Far West. The nearly universal appearance of these rites over this wide area in contrast to their absence in the east points to a common cultural heritage, at least in this practice, for western North America. Without assuming relative chronological sequences, the localized types are significant for the historical inferences that are to be drawn from the precisely defined linkages among those aggregations of cultures which may emerge as areally unique.[7] That these local types of girls' rites do not appear to coincide with the areal distinctions in shamanistic practices does not invalidate the suggestion of unique historically determined blocks of cultures. Such evidence may, if it continues to accumulate, indicate, however, that the conventional division into culture areas does not correspond to that culture history to be inferred from rigorous detailed comparisons of similarities.

The evidence indicating important local differentiations in institutions or in total cultures does not militate against the conception of the interrelationships in a larger basic area such as the ultramontane culture province suggested by Lowie. It is possible, however, that in these relatively simple cultures of western North America, especially in the Basin, the generalized basic traits that characterize such an area stand out more conspicuously than in the more highly organized and elaborated civilizations. This suggests that we are dealing here with elements or systems of culture which have been somewhat more stable than those elsewhere on the continent. If this is the case, the question of the stability of

[7] Spier, *Problems Arising from the Cultural Position of the Havasupai*, 218–219; *Klamath Ethnography*, 314–325.

these cultures has a wider significance which bears on problems of New World history. Thus it may be asked: Do the crude cultures of the Basin, perhaps also to a lesser degree those of neighboring areas, reflect substantially the customs of the first arrivals in the Western Hemisphere? Manifestly, it is impossible in those phases of culture that cannot be compared to the archaeological record to state precisely the relation to an ancient stratum. Still, the problem of cultural stability, as Lowie has pointedly suggested, is basic to the reconstruction of historical connections from the evidence of similarities.[8]

If it is assumed that many of the generalized shamanistic traits that appear widely in western North America, and in many instances extending even beyond this area, belong to an ancient stratum, it must also be recognized that a detailed comparison will often reveal significant local differences. Thus the Paviotso share with most North Americans the belief that supernatural power is derived from animal spirits. Whatever the local theory may be, the data show that in actual practice only a limited number of such beings are involved in shamanistic belief. Elsewhere, as in the northern Plateau, the shamans secure power from an indefinitely large group of people. On the other hand, among the upland Yumans to the south of the Basin, the number of animals that bestow power is more strictly limited than among the Paviotso. It must, therefore, be evident that the stability of culture inferred from the presence of generalized traits must rest upon full and detailed comparisons.

The problem of the relative stability of institutions, beliefs, and customs also figures prominently in the question of the relationships among the cultures of widely separated areas or continents. Nordenskiöld and Lowie have indicated suggestive similarities between elements in California-Basin and in some of the simpler South American cultures.[9] If it can be inferred from critical and sober comparisons that these resemblances are due to a genetic connection, the simple cultures of western North America should assume an important position in the reconstructions of

[8] Lowie, *Queries*, 288–290.

[9] Lowie has summarized these in the previously cited paper. Additional critical discussion of the intercontinental similarities and their significance is presented in his *Cultural Anthropology: A Science*, 310–315.

New World history. Unquestionably, detailed studies of Basin tribes and comparisons with surrounding cultures will yield rich evidence which should provide a basis for precise inferences of the degree of cultural stability in these cultures. This in turn should pave the way for an illuminating examination of the imposing South American parallels.

In addition to those linkages considered in the foregoing discussion, the distributional data of shamanistic practices reveal affiliations in still another quarter. The evidence of interrelationships in the shamanism of the Great Basin and some of the non-pueblo tribes on the Southwest is unmistakable. Similarities of the two regions include: a simple quest for power in caves in the mountains, a strong emphasis on dreaming as a direct causative agent in illness, and the prominence of dream experience in the acquisition of power. These are specific and positive resemblances which, moreover, figure prominently in the beliefs and practices of both areas. In addition to these, we find generalized traits in the two areas, shared, as Spier has indicated, with central California, and, in part, with the Plateau.[10]

The affiliations of the Basin with the non-pueblo tribes in the Southwest in the geographical outlay of localized groups of cultures, are far from simple. The exact relationship of Basin shamanism to Spier's Western Rancheria tribes is far from clear.[11] The heavy overlay of Pueblo features in Navaho and Western Apache obscures as yet whatever similarities to Basin shamanism may occur here. With the rest of this group, the upland Yumans of Arizona, similarities to Paviotso-Shoshoni practices are clearly evident. Again, however, the parallels are largely in striking likenesses in attitude and phrasing; the number of specific traits held in common does not appear to be large. These marked similarities between the Basin and the upland Yumans, taken in conjunction with evidence for resemblances in other phases of culture, make a strong case for an intimate relationship between the two areas.[12]

When we consider, however, those specific and far-reaching similarities mentioned above, important affiliations with still an-

[10] Spier, *Problems Arising from the Cultural Position of the Havasupai*, 216, Table I.
[11] Spier, *Op. cit.*, 214; *Cultural Relations of the Gila River and Lower Colorado Tribes*, 13.
[12] Spier, *Problems Arising from the Cultural Position of the Havasupai.*

other group of tribes come to the fore. These features do not figure so prominently in the shamanism of the upland Yumans, but they appear in full force in that province, recently delimited by Spier, embracing the Maricopa, Pima-Papago, and the Yumans of the lower Colorado river.[13] Unquestionably, these resemblances are significant, but a comparison of Paviotso-Shoshoni culture as a whole with the elements tabulated by Spier as characterizing the Gila-Lower Colorado area does not reveal the far-reaching correspondences that mark the upland Yuman and Basin situation.[14]

Perhaps detailed information on the southern Californian Shoshoneans might indicate a link through this region between the shamanism of the Gila-Colorado cultures and the Basin. In the face of the present paucity of data, particularly on shamanism, for these Shoshoneans, the suggestive similarities emerging from the distributional evidence remain puzzling. But they do tend to confirm the suggestion made earlier that the Paviotso-Shoshoni block of cultures is to be regarded as neither entirely unique nor dependent upon a single surrounding area. This carries the further implication, from the point of view of the classification of cultures into distinct areal types, that the connections to be inferred from detailed comparisons of similarities may not always coincide with such provinces; classification, in short, is not to be equated with history. It becomes increasingly evident, therefore, that the Basin in western North American cultures begins to assume a position somewhat different from the conception of this area as a hinterland receptive only to cultural impulses from central California.

The suggestion derived here from the distributional evidence of shamanistic belief and practice that the Great Basin and tribes of the non-pueblo Southwest are culturally linked is by no means novel. Spier has called attention on several occasions to the far-reaching similarities in both material and non-material aspects of life in the cultures of the upland Yumans and Basin peoples.[15]

---

[13] Spier, *Cultural Relations of the Gila River and Lower Colorado Tribes*, 12–14, 20–21.

[14] Spier, *Op. cit.*, 16–22. A comparison of the cultural features listed in this table with those tabulated in *Problems Arising from the Cultural Position of the Havasupai* bears out this contention.

[15] Spier, *Problems Arising from the Cultural Position of the Havasupai*. Distributional evidence of Havasupai-Basin affiliations is given in the comparative notes in *Havasupai Ethnography*.

Kroeber and Harrington have considered the problem archaeologically and see a northward extension into Nevada of Basket Maker culture. This conclusion is based on a number of similarities between Southwest Basket Maker and the material found in the lower levels of Lovelock Cave, which lies in the recent habitat of the Paviotso in Nevada.[16] If this larger Basket Maker area is confirmed by further archaeological investigation, the question of the relation of this culture to that of Western Rancheria-Paviotso remains unanswered. And obviously under the most favorable circumstances, only the relation of the material culture in the recent Basin and earlier Southwest can be determined. Time-sequences and connections in other phases of culture must remain futilely speculative.

It does, however, become increasingly clear that the affiliations in western North America cut across the conventional boundaries of culture areas. Moreover, it must be recognized that although many of the similarities upon which this conclusion is based are referrable to a common basic stock of generalized culture content, important interrelationships of localized blocks of cultures have resulted in far-reaching alterations of and additions to the widely occurring simple elements. Such a point of view does not ignore or deny the classificatory value of areal divisions into type cultures; it merely stresses the realities of the affiliations that are to be inferred from a detailed comparison of similarities.

This raises the question of what similarities in culture actually are. In the present study, resemblances in attitude, phrasing, and emphasis have been held to constitute as important evidence for historical inference of cultural connections as descriptively objective parts of culture. There is, of course, nothing new in this point of view, for ethnologists have long used evidence of these intangibles in reconstruction of history. Spier's studies, for example, have been imposing partially because of the way in which he has effectively scrutinized and employed the data of similarities of attitudes and phrasing in making historical reconstructions.[17]

---

[16] Kroeber, *Native Culture of the Southwest*, 383; Harrington in Loud and Harrington, *Lovelock Cave*, 120–123.

[17] The critical marshalling of such materials is found in all of Spier's work. It is for example, clearly apparent in his appraisal of the position of the Klamath in western North American cultures. *Klamath Ethnography*, 224 f.

Unquestionably, in shamanism resemblances in dominant viewpoints and in emphasis on particular beliefs or practices can be most satisfactorily explained by an inference of historical connection. The danger of conceptualizing similarities of this type where they do not exist is indeed great. Critical and detailed comparisons are demanded, however, no less in the use of other traits more descriptively isolable.

Still another perplexing problem in this study, as in any examination of the distribution of similarities, involves the selection and isolation of the units or the parts of the complex of the culture that are to be analyzed in their spatial relationships. Here there has been no attempt to treat traits as separate units on any *a priori* grounds. Certainly the only unitary nature possessed by culture elements comes from the actual events of history; the detachment of traits or clusters of traits from the original setting and the circumstances of diffusion. A culture complex such as the shamanistic charming of game at a communal drive involves a number of traits which, if diffused in this association, forms a unit from the strictly historical point of view. It would, therefore, be historically unjustified to break up this cluster into its component elements for separate distributional treatment. The question of unit traits is then resolved into the problem of first determining the actual history of the conditions under which specific elements of culture have clustered or separated. Isolating segments of culture as cultural units without this historical knowledge is based on *a priori* ethnological conceptualizing and as such may lead to misleading and indefensible inference of the past. It should be clearly evident, then, that the techniques employed in inferring the past must meet the difficulties of verifications and the realities of historical phenomena if ethnology is to be concerned with culture history and not speculations about history.

Bibliography

The following abbreviations are used:

AA	American Anthropologist
AAA-M	American Anthropological Association, Memoirs
AMNH-A	American Museum of Natural History, Anthropological Papers
AMNH-B	American Museum of Natural History, Bulletin
AMNH-M	American Museum of Natural History, Memoirs
BAE-B	Bureau of American Ethnology, Bulletin
BAE-R	Bureau of American Ethnology, Annual Report
JAFL	Journal of American Folk-Lore
UC-PAAE	University of California, Publications in American Archaeology and Ethnology
UW-PA	University of Washington, Publications in Anthropology
YUPA	Yale University Publications in Anthropology

Angulo, Jaime de.
    1926. The Background of the Religious Feeling in a Primitive Tribe. (AA 28, 352–360).
    1928. La Psychologie religieuse des Achomawi. (Anthropos 23, 141–166, 561–589).

Beaglehole, Ernest.
    1936. Hopi Hunting and Hunting Ritual. (YUPA No. 4).

Beals, Ralph L.
    1933. Ethnography of the Nisenan. (UC-PAAE 31, No. 6).

Benedict, Ruth Fulton.
    1922. The Vision in Plains Culture. (AA 24, 1–23).
    1923. The Concept of the Guardian Spirit in North America. (AAA-M No. 29).
    1924. A Brief Sketch of Serrano Culture. (AA 26, 366–392).

Boas, Franz.
    1923. Notes on the Tillamook. (UC-PAAE 20, 3–16).

Chamberlain, Alexander F.
    1901. Kootenay "Medicine Men." (JAFL 14, 95–99).

Chamberlin, Ralph V.
    1911. The Ethno-Botany of the Gosiute Indians of Utah. (AAA-M 2, Part 5).

Clements, Forrest E.
    1932. Primitive Concepts of Disease. (UC-PAAE 32, No. 2).

Cline, Walter B., Rachel S. Commons, May Mandelbaum, Richard H. Post, and L. W. V. Walters (edited by Leslie Spier).
    The Sinkaietk or Southern Okanagon of Washington.(MS. lent by Dr. Spier, of Yale University).

Cooke, Nan.
    Northern Ute Field Notes. (MS. lent by the author, who is now a graduate
        student at Yale University).
Curtis, Edward S.
    1907–30. The North American Indian. (Cambridge, Mass., 20 vols.).
Denig, Edwin T. (edited by J. N. B. Hewitt).
    1930. Indian Tribes of the Upper Missouri. (BAE-R 46, 375–628).
Densmore, Frances.
    1922. Northern Ute Music. (BAE-B 75).
    1929. Papago Music. (BAE-B 90).
    1932. Yuman and Yaqui Music. (BAE-B 110).
Dixon, Roland B.
    1904. Some Shamans of Northern California. (JAFL 17, 23–27).
    1905. The Northern Maidu. (AMNH-B 17, part 3).
    1907. The Shasta. (AMNH-B 17, part 5).
    1908. Notes on the Achomawi and Atsugewi Indians of Northern California.
        (AA 10, 208–220).
    1908. Some Aspects of the American Shaman. (JAFL 21, 1–12).
    1910. The Chimariko Indians and Language. (UC-PAAE 5, No. 5).
Du Bois, Constance Goddard.
    1908. The Religion of the Luiseño Indians of Southern California. (UC-
        PAAE 8, No. 3).
Du Bois, Cora A.
    1932. Tolowa Notes. (AA 34, 248–262).
    1935. Wintu Ethnography. (UC-PAAE 36, No. 1).
Emmons, George T.
    1911. The Tahltan Indians. (University of Pennsylvania Museum, An-
        thropological Publications 4, No. 1).
Forde, C. Daryll.
    1931. Ethnography of the Yuma Indians. (UC-PAAE 28, No. 4).
Freeland, L. S.
    1923. Pomo Doctors and Poisoners. (UC-PAAE 20, 57–73).
Gayton, A. H.
    1930. Yokuts-Mono Chiefs and Shamans. (UC-PAAE 24, No. 8).
    1935. Areal Affiliations of California Folktales. (AA 37, 589–599).
Gifford, Edward Winslow.
    1923. Western Mono Myths. (JAFL 36, 301–367).
    1927. Southern Maidu Religious Ceremonies. (AA 29, 214–257).
    1932. The Northfork Mono. (UC-PAAE 31, No. 2).
    1932. The Southeastern Yavapai. (UC-PAAE 29, No. 3).
    1933. The Cocopa. (UC-PAAE 31, No. 5).
Gifford, E. W., and Lowie, R. H.
    1928. Notes on the Akwa'ala Indians of Lower California. (UC-PAAE 23,
        No. 7).

Goddard, Pliny Earl.
    1903. Life and Culture of the Hupa. (UC-PAAE 1, No. 1).
Gunther, Erna.
    1926. Klallam Ethnography. (UW-PA 1, No. 5).
Haeberlin, Hermann.
    1918. SbEtEdáQ, A Shamanistic Performance of the Coast Salish. (AA 20, 249–257).
Harris, Jack.
    Shoshoni Field Notes. (MS. lent by the author, now a graduate student at Columbia University).
Hastings, James (ed.).
    1908. Encyclopaedia of Religion and Ethics. (New York, 13 vols.).
Hill, W. W.
    Navaho Field Notes. (MS. lent by the author, Assistant Professor of Anthropology at the University of New Mexico).
Hill-Tout, Charles.
    1902. Ethnological Studies of the Mainland Halkōmē'lEm, a division of the Salish of British Columbia. (Report of the Seventy-second Meeting of the British Association for the Advancement of Science).
Hodge, Frederick Webb (ed.).
    1907. Handbook of American Indians North of Mexico. (BAE-B 30, 2 vols.).
Hoebel, E. Adamson.
    Subjective Aspects of Shoshone Religion. (MS. lent by the author, Assistant Professor of Sociology at New York University).
Hooper, Lucille.
    1920. The Cahuilla Indians. (UC-PAAE 16, No. 6).
Hopkins, Sarah Winnemucca.
    1883. Life among the Piutes, Their Wrongs and Claims. (edited by Mrs. Horace Mann and Mary Tyler Mann, Boston, Mass.).
Kelly, Isabel T.
    1932. Ethnography of the Surprise Valley Paiute. (UC-PAAE 31, No. 3).
    1936. Chemehuevi Shamanism. (Essays in Anthropology Presented to A. L. Kroeber 129–142).
Kroeber, A. L.
    1907. The Arapaho. (AMNH-B 18).
    1907. The Religion of the Indians of California. (UC-PAAE 4, No. 6).
    1908. Ethnology of the Gros Ventre. (AMNH-A 1, part 4).
    1920. California Culture Provinces. (UC-PAAE 17, No. 2).
    1923. Anthropology. (New York).
    1923. American Culture and the Northwest Coast. (AA 25, 1–20).
    1925. Handbook of the Indians of California. (BAE-B 78).
    1928. Native Cultures of the Southwest. (UC-PAAE 23, No. 9).
    1929. The Valley Nisenan. (UC-PAAE 24, No. 4).
    1932. The Patwin and Their Neighbors. (UC-PAAE 29, No. 4).

Kroeber, A. L. (ed.), Fred Kniffen, Gordon MacGregor, Robert McKennan, Scudder Mekeel, and Maurice Mook.
    1935. Walapai Ethnography. (AAA-M No. 42).
Laufer, Berthold.
    1917. Origin of the Word Shaman. (AA 19, 361–371).
Loeb, Edwin M.
    1926. Pomo Folkways. (UC-PAAE 19, No. 2).
    1932. The Western Kuksu Cult. (UC-PAAE 33, No. 1).
Loud, Llewellyn L. and Harrington, M. R.
    1929. Lovelock Cave. (UC-PAAE 25, No. 1).
Lowie, Robert H.
    1909. The Northern Shoshone. (AMNH-AP 2, part 2).
    1922. The Religion of the Crow Indians. (AMNH-AP 25, part 2).
    1923. The Cultural Connection of Californian and Plateau Shoshonean Tribes. (UC-PAAE 20, 145–156).
    1924. Notes on Shoshonean Ethnography. (AMNH-AP 20, part 3).
    1924. Primitive Religion. (New York).
    1933. Queries. (AA 35, 288–296).
    1936. Cultural Anthropology: A Science. (The American Journal of Sociology 42, 301–320).
Mason, J. Alden.
    1912. The Ethnology of the Salinan Indians. (UC-PAAE 10, No. 4).
Murdock, G. P.
    Tenino Field Notes. (MS. lent by the author, Associate Professor of Anthropology at Yale University).
Natches, Gilbert.
    1923. Northern Paiute Verbs. (UC-PAAE 20, 245–259).
Nomland, Gladys Ayer.
    1935. Sinkyone Notes. (UC-PAAE 36, No. 2).
Opler, Marvin K.
    Southern Ute Field Notes. (MS. lent by the author, now a graduate student at Columbia University).
Park, Susan (Mrs. Willard Z.).
    Atsugewi Field Notes (MS.).
    Cahuilla Field Notes (MS.).
Park, Willard Z.
    1934. Paviotso Shamanism. (AA 36, 98–113).
Radin, Paul.
    1914. A Sketch of the Peyote Cult of the Winnebago: A Study in Borrowing. (Journal of Religious Psychology 7, 1–22).
    1915. Religion of the North American Indians. (Anthropology in North America, by Franz Boas [and others], New York, 259–305).
    1933. The Method and Theory of Ethnology. (New York).

Ray, Verne F.
  1932. The Sanpoil and Nespelem, Salishan Peoples of Northeastern Washington. (UW-PA 5).
Russell, Frank.
  1908. The Pima Indians. (BAE-R 26, 3–389).
Sapir, Edward.
  1907. Religious Ideas of the Takelma Indians of Southwestern Oregon. (JAFL 20, 33–49).
  1916. Time Perspective in Aboriginal American Culture. A Study in Method. (Canada Department of Mines Geological Survey Anthropological Series Memoir 90, No. 13).
    Hupa Ethnological Notes (MS. lent by the author, Professor of Anthropology at Yale University).
    Kaibab Field Notes (MS. lent by the author, Professor of Anthropology at Yale University).
Spier, Leslie.
  1923. Southern Diegueño Customs. (UC-PAAE 20, 297–358).
  1928. Havasupai Ethnography. (AMNH-AP 29, part 3).
  1929. Problems Arising from the Cultural Position of the Havasupai. (AA 31, 213–222).
  1930. Klamath Ethnography. (UC-PAAE 30).
  1933. Yuman Tribes of the Gila River. (Chicago).
  1935. The Prophet Dance of the Northwest and its Derivatives: The Source of the Ghost Dance. (General Series in Anthropology, No. 1, New Haven).
  1936. Cultural Relations of the Gila River and Lower Colorado Tribes. (YUPA No. 3).
Spier, L., and Sapir, E.
  1930. Wishram Ethnography. (UW-PA 3, No. 3).
Spinden, Herbert J.
  1908. The Nez Percé Indians. (AAA-M 2, part 3).
Steward, Julian H.
  1933. Ethnography of the Owens Valley Paiute. (UC-PAAE 33, No. 3).
Strong, William Duncan.
  1929. Aboriginal Society in Southern California. (UC-PAAE 26).
Teit, James.
  1900. The Thompson Indians of British Columbia. (AMNH-M 2, part 4).
  1906. The Lillooet Indians. (AMNH-M 4, part 5).
  1909. The Shuswap. (AMNH-M 4, part 7).
Wissler, Clark.
  1915. The Material Cultures of the North American Indians. (Anthropology in North America, by Franz Boas [and others], New York, 76–134).
  1922. The American Indian. (New York).

Index of Tribal Names